Listening
for God in
Contemporary
Fiction

THE EMMAUS READERS

Edited by
Susan M. Felch
and
Gary D. Schmidt

PARACLETE PRESS
Brewster, Massachussetts

The Emmaus Readers: Listening for God in Contemporary Fiction

2008 First Printing

Copyright © 2008 by Susan M. Felch and Gary D. Schmidt

ISBN: 978-1-55725-543-3

All Scriptures quotations, unless otherwise noted, are taken from the Revised Standard Version of the Bible, © 1952 [2nd edition, 1971] by the Division of Christian Education of the National Council of Churches of Christ in the USA. Used by permission. All rights reserved.

Library of Congress Cataloging-in-Publication Data
The Emmaus readers : listening for God in contemporary fiction / edited by Susan M. Felch and Gary D. Schmidt.
        p. cm.
  Includes bibliographical references.
  Twelve contemporary works of fiction of various genres (historical fiction, science fiction, mystery, thriller, etc.) and of various religious traditions. Includes guides, discussions and questions.
  ISBN: 978-1-55725-543-3
  1. Religious fiction, American. 2. Religious fiction, English. 3. American fiction—20th century. 4. English fiction—20th century. 5. Spirituality in literature. 6. Fiction—Pschycological aspects. I. Felch, Susam M., 1951- II. Schmidt, Gary D.
  PS648.R44E66 2008
  823'.914080382—dc22   2007052561

10 9 8 7 6 5 4 3 2 1

Published by Paraclete Press
Brewster, Massachusetts
www.paracletepress.com
Printed in the United States of America

Contents

Introduction

I have three books on the desk beside me as I am writing this introduction. Really. There they sit.

The first is one you may never have heard of: *The Little World of Don Camillo*, by Giovanni Guareschi. Written soon after World War II, it is set in a tiny town in the valley of the Po River, where Don Camillo is the local parish priest and Peppone is the local Communist mayor. As you may imagine, there is a continuous sparring between them, a sparring of which Christ, to whom Don Camillo speaks on the crucifix above the altar, sometimes approves and sometimes disapproves. At first comic, the sparring becomes more and more serious—particularly after the mischievous Don Camillo has Peppone's son sing before the bishop. In fact, toward the close of the novel, Don Camillo is almost assassinated—a possibility which terrifies not Don Camillo, but Peppone, who is, in many ways, as close a friend as a parish priest is likely to have.

In the last scene, Peppone comes to visit Don Camillo—secretly. Don Camillo is repainting the animals for the Nativity set, and instinctively Peppone sits down and begins to help. He paints the figure of the Holy Infant. Don Camillo sits on the other side of the table, a bright light between them, and by the end of their talk, Don Camillo has laid his finger on the ass and identified it as Peppone, who has laid his own finger on the ox and identified it as Don Camillo. Then, in perfect understanding, they sit and listen as silence comes over their world, and it is the silence of peace.

Thirty-five years have gone by since I first read that scene. Thirty-five years, and I remember the chill that went through me, the sense that something true and noble and real and deeply spiritual, almost numinous, had been spoken. So when I found the novel in a used bookshop—a lousy dog-eared, coverless reprint for a couple of bucks—I bought it with the sense that I had found something beyond price.

The second book on the desk is *Inherit the Wind* by Jerome Lawrence and Robert E. Lee, a first edition and first printing, which I also found in a used bookshop and which really was almost beyond price. I hadn't been looking for it particularly, but as soon as I saw it on the shelf, the final scene leapt back to me as though I had just finished the play. The drama is a fictionalized account of the Scopes Monkey Trials, in which Clarence Darrow and William Jennings Bryan debated the merits of a Tennessee law against the teaching of evolution. When the trial is over, Henry Drummond—the character who represents Darrow—is confronted by E.K. Hornbeck, who scoffs at the unthinking way Christians have dismissed Charles Darwin. Drummond, however, refuses Hornbeck's easy cynicism.

Left alone in the courtroom, he notices Rachel Brown's copy of Darwin's *The Origin of Species*. He picks it up and walks to the judge's bench, where he also picks up the Bible sitting there. And then—and I remember reading this as vividly as if I had read it this morning—he holds the two, balances them thoughtfully, half-smiles, and slaps them together. Quietly he leaves the courtroom, crosses the street, and exits the stage through an empty town square—the two stories side by side in his briefcase.

The third is an early edition of J.R.R. Tolkien's *The Hobbit*. According to the penciled inscription written on the map, right by the Lonely Mountain where Smaug rules, the book was given to Betsy from Mummy and Daddy for Christmas, 1949. I wonder how she could bear to have lost it. I rescued this from a bookshop in Salem, Massachusetts, a shop which specialized in Wiccan books and paraphernalia and yet which had, sitting in its front window when I walked by, this slight green book which I had not looked at since I was in junior high.

Seven years have gone by since I bought it, and this is the first summer where, when I pick it up, it does not still reek of the incense that wafted over it while in Salem. When I read its closing lines, as Bilbo comes to understand that perhaps he, even he, might have had a hand in the prophecies of the old songs coming true, I am glad I bought it, because I remember the thrill I felt that first time, when it suddenly seemed altogether possible that, in fact, even a small boy might play some sort of role in the grand game.

Stories matter. In a world where language is manipulated to make the glitzy seem golden, stories matter. In a world where language is contorted to make power seem benign, to make aggression seem like peace, to make self-interest seem like altruism, stories matter. In a world where language can be redefined to make it seem that reality itself is only an infinitely adjustable name, stories matter.

Stories matter. They can speak truth. When a parish priest and a Communist mayor find peace while painting Nativity figures, when Henry Drummond holds two approaches to the realities of this world and slaps them together, when Bilbo Baggins recognizes that even a tiny hobbit might play a large role in the universe—or, to put it in other words, when readers learn these truths: that love is of God; that the Lord our God, the Lord is one; and that while we consider the vastness of all the works of God's fingers, we can know that God is mindful of even the smallest individual—we know that stories matter, and that they speak truth.

In his *Apology for Poetry*, written during the Renaissance, Sir Philip Sidney argued that truth can come through history—the recitation of fact—and it can come through philosophy—the discussion of abstract truth. But, he argued, these are only brass worlds. Beautiful, but still only brass. The work of the poet—by which

Sidney would have included the teller of stories—is a golden world, because in creating story, the poet creates an entire world, an aesthetically beautiful world, by which the writer can speak true things, enabling readers such as ourselves to understand more fully, more deeply, and passionately than we might have understood were we confronted with only brass.

But gold in books, like gold under ground, is not easily or lightly found.

Sidney spoke to a culture which he assumed would read with spiritual eyes. It was a world that began with the assumption that everything was responding to the spiritual, and that to live was to respond to the spiritual. How could you look at the moon, which waxes and wanes, and not see beyond to the fixed realm of the eternal stars, and know that something deeply spiritual was being spoken? How could you look at the slug, and not see how far beneath you it seems, and how far above it you are, and how far above you are the orders of angels, and God himself?

But Sidney's assumption is long gone in our culture, and we no longer read easily with spiritual eyes. It may not occur to us. Or we may lack the inclination. Or we may simply have lost the vocabulary with which to think about spiritual insights. Or we may not recognize them when they appear in ways that are unfamiliar, embedded, say, in a work of fiction. Or we may have simply bought into the notion that fiction is only storytelling, and telling a story is telling something that is not true. So why read with spiritual eyes, when the thing you are reading is, by definition, not true?

Because the definition is wrong. Because story matters. Because those feelings, that sense that something very real and true had been spoken when I turned the pages of *The Little World of Don Camillo* and *Inherit the Wind* and *The Hobbit* or when you turned the pages of books that you remember and felt what I felt—what

E.M. Forster called the "queer prickings of delight"—come in moments when we recognize that we have been confronted spiritually, and we will not be the same again.

In the summer of 2006, nine friends gathered to see what might be gained by purposefully and explicitly reading a set of novels through spiritual eyes. And so the Emmaus Readers were born as a group of fellow Christians, spiritual seekers all of us, teaching and working at Calvin College, who felt drawn to the questions of how faith might affect the ways to read and understand fiction. The nine of us met together for a year—once a month during the summer and every two weeks during the school year—to talk about the twelve novels we'd selected, grappling and wrestling with what they might say to us; listening, as the first two disciples on the road to Emmaus listened, for the often surprising spiritual insights that come from paying close attention to stories. Although not every writer shared our faith commitments, we recognized the truths that each brought to light, and we learned to push beyond our immediate likes and dislikes to the deeper satisfactions a well-crafted tale provides.

For this volume, the Emmaus Readers have gathered together twelve contemporary works of fiction. They span various genres—historical fiction, science fiction, realism, mystery, thriller, a saint's life, a graphic novel, a contemporary western, fantasy. They span various countries—the United States, Great Britain, Canada. They span various religious traditions—Anglican, Catholic, Jewish, Presbyterian, and—if this is a tradition—agnosticism. And they span very different ways of approaching the task of creating the golden world.

These works of fiction are united, however, in this: each of the novels wants to confront its readers with questions that are deeply spiritual in nature. They ask to be read with spiritual eyes. To ignore these confrontations is to cheapen the read, to not enter fully into the golden world the novelists have formulated. To ignore Mr. Ives' confrontation with the sacred vision in the midst of spiritual doubt; to not take seriously Reuben Land's claim that he has been there and is going back—make of it what you will; to not struggle with an assassin's penitence and with his son's guilt; to pass over the shriveling of Dottie's spirit through its insistence on its own way; to cheapen Father Emilio Sandoz' pain by missing its spiritual dimension—well, all of this is possible, but you as reader would not have been confronted with the spiritual issues that loom in these books. You have missed the golden world.

The guides and discussions and questions in this volume are meant to prompt and to prod. They are not meant to suggest that these are the only ways of reading these books, that here are the right answers, or that all that needs to be said has been said. They are guides to thinking about these novels with spiritual eyes— meaning that they try to draw out the ways in which writers are confronting readers with the deepest matters of the spirit. The synopsis for each book will give you an overview of the novel, perhaps before you've even picked it up, and the page numbers refer to the editions that are listed in the bibliography. But the section titled "Considering the Novel" assumes that you have read it for yourself and invites you into a conversation about the ending—as well as the beginning and middle—of the novel. These discussions, then, are not substitutes for reading the works themselves; that would be confusing the pick and shovel for the gold. They are, instead, the musings of a group of readers like yourself, who have come together now for a couple of years, trying to mine the deep gold of these golden worlds.

We're glad you've joined us.

Under the Mercy, we hope you'll never be the same.

It Is Well with My Soul

When peace, like a river, attendeth my way,
When sorrows like sea billows roll;
Whatever my lot, Thou has taught me to say,
It is well, it is well, with my soul.

It is well, with my soul,
It is well, with my soul,
It is well, it is well, with my soul.

Though Satan should buffet, though trials should come,
Let this blest assurance control,
That Christ has regarded my helpless estate,
And hath shed His own blood for my soul.

My sin, oh, the bliss of this glorious thought!
My sin, not in part but the whole,
Is nailed to the cross, and I bear it no more,
Praise the Lord, praise the Lord, O my soul!

And Lord, haste the day when my faith shall be sight,
The clouds be rolled back as a scroll;
The trump shall resound, and the Lord shall descend,
Even so, it is well with my soul.

—*Horatio G. Spafford, 1873*

PART ONE

"When Sorrows Like
Sea Billows Roll"

"When Sorrows Like Sea Billows Roll"

In the beginning of his somewhat grim novel, *Jude the Obscure*, Thomas Hardy pictures the young Jude longing for the heavenly city—here defined as the small town of Christminster. He waits in a path, clutching a grammar, despairing because he cannot understand it, and believing that because he cannot understand it, he must be unworthy of a town such as Christminister. Hardy writes that if someone had come along just then, as if in answer to Jude's deepest longings, all might have been well. "But," Hardy writes, "nobody did come, because nobody does." No one is listening at all.

This notion—that nobody comes, that nobody is listening, that God himself does not respond to our pleas—this is a notion that contemporary novelists explore as well, as they craft characters who grieve in a world that is filled with brokenness, loneliness, pain, and cruelty. The search for an other, the search for a community, the search for God—all these echo characters' searches for meaning and fulfillment—searches which are often desperate, and which take on the tonalities of hopelessness. The characters in Ron Hansen's *Mariette in Ecstasy*, P.D. James's *The Children of Men*, and Mary Doria Russell's *The Sparrow* and *The Children of God* all ask the kinds of questions that Hardy raises, all looking for ways to feel that there is more than the self—that there is God's hand, that there is meaning and beauty and love, despite all the evidence of this broken world. How does one understand what seems to be a call from God, Hansen and Russell both ask, when that call can be accompanied by utter loss and abandonment? How does one think about hope in a world where there seems to be no reason at all to hope? asks P.D. James. Is there joy? Is there love? Is there meaning?

MARIETTE IN ECSTASY Ron Hansen
(1991)

Synopsis

When Mariette Baptiste enters the Couvent de Notre-Dame
des Afflictions in New York at age seventeen in order to
join the Sisters of the Crucifixion, she is welcomed already
as someone who is bright, pretty, devout, and admirable.
Though her father disagrees with her decision to join
the convent—having already given one daughter to the
sisters—Mariette enters gladly, and almost immediately
her decision seems to be confirmed by a series of religious
ecstasies that become the talk of the convent. As the months
go by, these ecstasies become more intense, more frequent,
and are joined by the presence of the stigmata, the wounds
of Christ on Mariette's hands, feet, and side—their first
presentation appearing on the day after her sister's death.
The sisters become bitterly divided over Mariette's presence,
some believing her to be saintly, some believing that the
signs are fraudulent, some accusing her of theatricals,
some of being self-deluded. But even the criticism seems
to confirm Mariette's sense that she would be scorned and
abandoned—a prophecy which comes true when her father,
who is a physician, examines the wounds in the presence of
her religious superiors and pronounces them a trick. Though
her superiors will not say that the presentations and ecstasies
are fraudulent, Mariette is, in the end, sent away from the
convent because the sisters consider her an overwhelmingly
disruptive force to their tranquility.

On the Author

Ron Hansen (b. 1947), a native of Omaha, Nebraska, and a veteran of the Vietnam War, began his writing career by authoring westerns—*Desperadoes* (1979) and *The Assassination of Jesse James by the Coward Robert Ford* (1983)—and a collection of short fiction about his home state, *Nebraska* (1989), which earned the American Academy and Institute of Arts and Letters Award in Literature. But in 1991, he turned sharply away from that genre and wrote *Mariette in Ecstasy*, basing his novel on the life of Thérèse of Lisieux (1872–97), and examining in his prose the spiritual life of characters in strikingly lyrical and profound ways. He combined these interests in his next novel, *Atticus* (1996), an unsettling retelling of the story of the prodigal son, which became a finalist for the National Book Award. His recent collection, *A Stay Against Confusion: Essays on Faith and Fiction* (2001), explores this turning and his own understanding of the role of his Catholic faith in his writing. Having as a student taken his MFA from the University of Iowa, he is now a teacher of writing as the Gerard Manley Hopkins SJ Professor of the Arts and Humanities at Santa Clara University.

Considering the Novel

Mariette in Ecstasy begins with a series of poetic, haunting, and evocative images that seem to function as the opening shots of a film: they establish setting, and they slowly direct the reader's eye to details of the natural world first—"Wallowing beetles in green pond water" (3), then to suggestions of the human presence in that world—"Wooden reaper. Walking plow. Hayrick" (3), then to more concrete and immediate evidence of that presence—"Tallow candles in red glass jars shudder on a high altar" (4), and then, finally, to the characters who will inhabit the story—"Sister Sabine is in a jean apron as she strolls toward the milking barn" (5). Set in the present tense, the details are very immediate, very real, very specific, and Hansen returns to such listings throughout the novel, as if to suggest to the reader that the contemplative and perhaps mystical lives of the Sisters of the Crucifixion, whose prayers and purposes seem so otherworldly, are in fact rooted in the very present and immediate world. The beautiful concrete images of the world—the garden, the sunlight, the hayfields, the night sky, the timothy grass—suggest a way of grasping the world itself, in all its beauty and concreteness. There is the contemplation of Christ's crucifixion, and there are the Guernsey cows to be milked. There are the psalms to be recited, and there are the white sheets and undergarments to be hung. The mundane is placed beside the sacred—though the lyrical writing elevates even the mundane toward exceptional beauty. Is this a metaphor for what the sacred may do to the mundane as well?

The novel's opening also firmly suggests the intense ordering of this world. Hansen begins with a "Directoire des Religieuses du Couvent de Notre-Dame des Afflictions," and so lists each of the sisters and the one postulant, her age, and her responsibilities, as though the entire community can be rigorously ordered and defined. This is immediately followed by "The Winter Life of the Sisters of the Crucifixion," presenting the daily schedule of the sisters, whose lives are planned very closely—again, a rigorous ordering. And the story itself continues this pattern, as much of the text is divided according to the days of the saints, tying all of the sisters' activities tightly to the liturgical calendar. This is a world, Hansen suggests, where there is little surprise, little spontaneity; all is order and expectation. Hansen shows a practical group, a highly organized social entity.

Even the most intense acts of spiritual devotion find their rhythm within the ordering of the mundane and the sacred. Mother

Saint-Raphaël prunes the roses, but she also takes the thorns and fastens them around herself so that they will pierce and infect her skin—and so bring her into union with the suffering of Christ. But Mariette's entrance into the novel quickly disturbs all of this rigorous order and mangles all of the expectations of this social entity. She seems to disturb and undercut the sisters' spirituality by leaving the immediate world around her and becoming insensible to it, entering mystical spheres that the other sisters seem unable to reach. She pits the immediate world of the senses against a mystical union with Christ. Mother Saint-Raphaël "winces and shuts her eyes" (6) when she tightens the rose prunings, closing off sight but not pain, but Mariette seems entirely absent from her body in a mystical and otherworldly ecstasy. Hansen poses the same question to the reader that the convent asks itself: is Mariette's spirituality a stronger, more authentic experience?

Certainly the sisters embrace a spirituality that focuses on the body and on their unity with Christ's suffering; this spirituality affirms the value of physical suffering as a spiritual discipline and as a way of identifying with Christ. Mother Céline delights, for example, in the presence of the tumor that will eventually kill her. (Thérèse of Lisieux died from "galloping tuberculosis," an acute state that affects the entire body, leading to great physical suffering; Thérèse called this a "martyrdom"—by which she meant a giving of the self completely to God.) But there is a sense of balance among the sisters as well. There is the ordinary work to do, and there are the stolen moments of gossip and laughter, and there is food to be eaten—albeit in silence. But Mariette's arrival at the convent changes this balance between the spiritual impulse toward suffering and the spiritual discipline of living in the ordinary world; Mariette institutes a spectacular spirituality, and if the lives of the sisters had before been situated midway on a continuum between the mystical and the ordinary—both of which are a part of their spiritual lives—their lives are now pushed dramatically, almost chaotically toward the mystical.

Mariette brings with her an ecstatic devotional life that seems to have no place in the disciplined, liturgically ordered schedule of the other sisters' devotional lives. A schedule highlighted by the rigors of sleeplessness and silence and cold and penitence seems to have no place for accepting the surprise that Mariette brings, and so it is not long before Mariette is seen as an enormously disruptive influence on the life of the convent. Eventually, her presence will even test the faith of her Mother Superior, who cannot understand why God would bring such a problem into their world, and who finds herself moved to hate Mariette and to feel jealousy over the quality of Mariette's religious vocation. Why, in a cloistered life which is chastened by obedience, would God introduce disorder?

Hansen refuses to create a narrative that shows an easy answer to this question, but he does direct readers quite forcefully to the sisters' responses to Mariette. Here we see a community of contemplatives who are separated out of the world in order to serve Christ dutifully and fully—yet they are still forced to confront the very real presence of the sinful soul. Some of the sisters are authentically moved by Mariette's devotion. One sees Mariette as the highlight of her religious vocation; another speaks of Mariette as "a sacrament." Others are vexed by envy, either of the quality of her devotion, or by the ways in which she is regarded by others in the community, or, perhaps, by the intimacy of her relationship with Christ. Some are moved toward real hatred, seeing in Mariette impulses that they themselves have fought against, and some even see Mariette as a deliberate trickster whose goal is attention, a special setting apart that might cause dissension in the community. Some are moved to vile accusations—even against Henri Marriott, the priest who serves the community—while others are moved to affirmation: "Oh, what a happiness to have had such a blessed woman amongst us! I, for one, can affirm that the whole time Mariette has been here, never once has the tiniest trouble arisen in the sisterhood on her account, nor did I ever notice any defect in her, I say no defect, not even smallest" (142)—though, as Mariette herself reminds the sisters, the first syllable of her name means "flaw" (15).

Certainly a central focus in the novel is Hansen's exploration of the community dynamics of the Sisters of the Crucifixion. Here is a sisterhood devoted to contemplation of the sufferings of Christ and to cultivating a desire to share mystically in those sufferings. But, shows Hansen, even nuns cannot leave their sinful nature behind them. "We don't hurry; we don't worry; we try not to wrestle too much with our inner torments and petty irritations" (67), Sister Saint-Denis tells Mariette (this immediately after Mariette has imagined Sister Saint-Denis playing the role of Santa Claus). But the whole novel is filled with tales of inner torments and petty irritations that are hidden behind innocuous requests for penance for such sins as being too loud while walking in the hallways and shutting doors. When Sister Dominique confesses to poor attention in her late-night devotions, her sin is immediately trumped by Sister Saint-Léon. As Sister Dominique acidly points out: "[Y]ou have undervalued even my sins" (86). Hansen tells us no more about this apparently bitter relationship, but it stands as an emblem of the hidden tensions that mark the relationships in the community—tensions which are heightened when the community begins to divide in its responses to Mariette's presence.

While it is these vast differences that cause the Mother Superior to question why God would bring Mariette to the convent, the reader sees a very human set of responses to the exceptional and the extraordinary, responses ranging from joy at God's gifts to envy at what seems to be God's slights. "She is who I was meant to be," laments one sister, and the reader is led to the question, Can God provide the calling yet not provide the gifts and skills to fulfill that calling? Mother Saint-Raphaël, as she is about to dismiss Mariette from the convent, assures her, "God sometimes wants our desire for a religious vocation but not the deed itself" (174)—a cold comfort to the forlorn Mariette and a hard saying to any Christian. It also suggests Mother Saint-Raphaël's sense of compromise; in the end, she believes in the miracles that swirl around Mariette, but she must act as though she does not for the larger peace of the community. One senses the spiritual harm of such a compromise.

Hansen does not allow the reader simply to observe the responses of the sisters; the reader, too, is called to make a judgment about Mariette's ecstasies and presentations. Are the ecstasies and stigmata actually given to her? Or has she, in the words of Mother Saint-Raphaël, "helped the experience"? There is evidence on both sides. Mariette does move into authentic ecstasies, and the witnesses of these moments affirm that her mystical experiences are genuine. During these experiences, she is tested with pins and forks and flames—and she never fails the test. The bleeding from the stigmatic wounds is abnormally contained. When she is interviewed about these experiences, the Mother Superior begins with a question designed to irritate Mariette toward confession, but she passes that test as well. There is real blood, and there are real wounds as large as pennies, and there are witnesses to both. There are signs—and witnesses—that Mariette does battle with demons. One contemplative and ecstatic scene is entirely within Mariette's own consciousness, and Hansen suggests no sign of her dissembling—unless she is utterly unconscious of it herself. And there is the external evidence of her blood on a handkerchief belonging to Father Marriott, blood which scents his entire room with the powerful smell of lilies; there are two witnesses to this miracle. Both Father Marriott, who has been inclined to believe her, and Mother Saint-Raphaël, who has been inclined to disbelieve her, affirm the truth of the experience, even though it can never be proven: "God gives us just enough to seek Him, and never enough to fully find him. To do more would inhibit our freedom, and our freedom is very dear to God" (174).

But there is, on the other hand, evidence as well that Mariette's presentations are, as some of the sisters claim, fraudulent. As Hansen directs the reader's eye to various concrete and seemingly mundane details around the convent, he points out scissors that Mariette holds, sharp wires, and a loose nail in a plank in the floor of her cell—instruments that could be used to fake the stigmata. When she first comes to the convent, she listens to readings from Julian of Norwich that speak of an intimacy and identification with Christ in his suffering—an identification for which, Mariette admits, she herself prays. Has this passage suggested the presentations to her? There is a vial of dried blood which, under certain conditions, becomes liquid again, and a reference to a waterproofing agent that might protect simulated wounds from washings. Before the stigmata appear, Mariette has been studying the phenomenon in church history and theology, almost as if preparing herself to stage the event. The very public nature of Mariette's ecstasies makes it seem that they are almost staged, awaiting the proper audience, which is always available, and which provides a witness and indeed a persona for Mariette. It is a persona that sets her apart.

In one section—immediately before the "Mass of the Presentation of the Blessed Virgin Mary"—Mariette actually participates in a staged "playlet," performing the part of the Beloved from the *Song of Songs*; here, and elsewhere, sensuousness is at the heart of her spirituality. Though some of the Sisters feel that the sensuality of the playlet is inappropriate, Mariette shows no sense of this: "Let my Beloved come into his garden, let him taste its precious fruits" (83). Her use of the *Song of Songs's* images links erotic desire with a spiritual love of Christ, a link which is made explicit when she acts out the role of the abandoned lover who yearns to tell her bridegroom that she is "sick with love" (85), following which she kneels in homage to Christ on the cross. The linkage of love for Christ with erotic imagery appears frequently to describe Mariette's spirituality; even in her childhood play with the younger Annie, she is encouraged to give herself wholly to Jesus, a request that she accepts by saying, "Yes, I told her; yes and yes a hundred times" (74). And the book is bracketed by scenes of Mariette admiring her own body in the mirror, noting that even this physical beauty she will give to Christ (9, 178). This kind of imagery is connected to no other character, and at times it clearly disturbs the other sisters, despite the scriptural connections. "We shouldn't be doing this," says Sister Philomène of the playlet, and she is troubled when Sister Hermance nudges her "with gusto" (83) during the acting. Later, when Mariette describes her ecstasies in explicitly sexual terms—"When he tells me to sleep, I do so at once, and he holds me. And I share in him as if he's inside me. And he is" (168)—Mother Saint-Raphaël's response is to slap Mariette "harshly."

More disturbing is the suggestion that the line between religious ecstasy and madness may be very fine indeed. When she first reveals the wounds of the stigmata to Father Marriott, Mariette has come barefoot from the church across the wintry path. She walks "falteringly" (112), leaving blood with every step. "She holds out her blood-painted hands like a present and she smiles crazily as she says, 'Oh, look at what Jesus has done to me!'" (112). Has Mariette's devotion at this point moved her toward what we might call a clinical insanity? Or is what might appear to be insanity to an outside observer an entrance into an extreme spirituality? Mariette herself wonders this; in one of her letters, she complains that Jesus has withdrawn from her, leaving her barren. "The sheer insanity of love has never been worse than this" (75), she writes. But Mariette is certainly not speaking here of clinical illness, and Sister Catherine, who listens to this letter read aloud, refuses to accept the notion that Mariette is insane: "She is passionate. . . . She is *not* hysterical" (75). But neither Sister Catherine nor Ron Hansen gives any indication how the distinctions between authentic passion and clinical hysteria are to be drawn—perhaps in Mariette, these are positions on a continuum. One way to read the presentations and ecstasies is to define them as authentic, Hansen suggests; another way may be to define them as religious madness—and Hansen allows for this possibility, too. But Hansen—who is always asking readers to understand why they may be responding as they do—also hints that readers might be inclined to lean toward a more rational, clinical explanation of Mariette's spirituality because the rational is the safe alternative to choose; to say otherwise—to say that what seems madness is indeed legitimate and real spiritual communion—is almost frightening, and we readers might prefer to stand with the sisters in a safe and controlled spirituality.

It may be, as well, that Mariette is working out the effects of abuse, as there are several suggestions in the novel that her father may have sexually assaulted her. She is certainly more than a little fearful of him, and the demonic rape scene, which Mariette first interprets as a nighttime dream, and then not as a dream, may be a re-enactment of a real scene or scenes with her father. When she tends to her sister in her father's presence, Mariette "feels his eyes like hands. Enjoying her. She knows their slow travel and caress" (97). These are only hints, but if such were the case, then Mariette could well be turning her spiritual—and sexual—response toward a purer source, and, at the same time, seeking the convent as a safe place from her father, and a place within which to exercise this other purer love.

So Hansen provides the reader with several alternatives in evaluating Mariette: she may be sincere but deluded, or she may be sincere and dissimulating, or she may be sincere and the signs and presentations all authentic. Perhaps all of these are in part true. Or perhaps Mariette comes to the convent with the humble recognition that she is a flawed person on a spiritual journey. Her name, she tells Sister Agnès, is "Mar-iette, like a flaw" (15). Is it her real sense of her own humble spiritual state that drives and goads her toward what she sees as a more perfect spiritual state—a spiritual state which makes some of the sisters envious or suspicious?

But however the reader understands Mariette and her motivations, and however the reader interprets the reality of the signs that are associated with her, clearly Mariette is a young woman who wants to love Christ. The manifestations of that love may be complicated, and the responses toward her manifestations may be complicated, but the complications do not negate the real belief, the real yearning that Mariette exhibits. Her desire seems quite real and pure—even if that purity is fractured by the complications of the real world. Perhaps, suggests Hansen, pure desire may be real, but in the crucible of the world, pure desire for God cannot be enacted purely. "Don't try to be exceptional; simply be a good nun" (31), the Reverend Mother tells Mariette. But in advancing this formula, has the Reverend Mother assured Mariette of a mediocre, easy, familiar, and rather plain spiritual life? Is this enough? Mariette suggests that it is not.

Into this mix Hansen places Father Henri Marriott, who is the first witness of the stigmata, and Dr. Baptiste. Father Marriott is an old priest who is coming to the end of his priesthood; he is tended by several of the sisters, who clean his house and provide food and lay out his clothing for him. But in general he is outside their immediate community, not embroiled in the inner turmoils and petty irritations of their world; the stakes in terms of relationships are not nearly as high for him as for the sisters. He, like the reader, stands apart. He institutes the formal examination of Mariette's case to determine the veracity of her stigmata and he is convinced. The smell of the lilies has already proven to him the truthfulness of her experience, and his letters affirm his faith in Mariette. He is actually eager to believe. In his letters, Père Marriott admits the possibility that this is "all a phantasy" (148). But he insists that Mariette's character affirms the reality of her experience. The real difficulty for Father Marriott is Mariette's challenge to the conventional. "We are bored and dull and tired of each other, and we have such a yearning for some sign from God that this matters, that our prayers and good works are important to him" (148), he writes. For Père Marriott, Mariette is that longed-for sign, and when Dr. Baptiste scornfully claims that Mariette has duped them, Père Marriott insists that even the disappearance of the wounds is miraculous—a response that draws disdain from Dr. Baptiste, whose own faith in science leads him to consider those who believe in miracles as merely credulous. Hansen gives no further response from Père Marriott; Mariette apparently leaves the convent without ever having another word with or from him. In this silence, Hansen leaves open the equally strong possibilities that the priest will believe in the signs despite the evidence, or he will not believe and his faith that God affirms his work will be shattered.

Dr. Baptiste, the skeptic, is also outside the community, separated by a grill from his two daughters who have embraced the spiritual world of the sisters. Dr. Baptiste is always associated with his medical competence, but in addition, he is associated with the larger world by the many references to concrete details about his person: the blood on his cuffs, medicinal scents, and his array of coats, which the narrator never fails to mention. The doctor dismisses Mariette's spiritual life as excessive and irrational: "She is always saying preposterous things; that's why we don't get along" (173), he announces. He is known as someone who always denies and explains away the miraculous, and so, when Mariette is brought to him for examination, she asks, "Are you trying to turn it into a disease?" (171)—which is exactly the kind of rational response she expects from her father, who is "as firm and practical as a clock" (173). She is not surprised, it seems, when the stigmata disappear in his presence; he, too, is not surprised, though for a different reason.

Hansen maintains a tight point of view and does not reveal to the reader many of Mariette's inner thoughts. When he does, he leaves the very strong possibility that Mariette does not herself realize that her thoughts may not be authentic. Perhaps Mariette is quite conscious of her role and is very carefully having the sisters see her in the way that she wants to be seen. Perhaps the spare voice of the novel suggests that readers, too, are seeing Mariette only as she wants to be seen. Then again it may be true that Mariette is absolutely authentic in all of her spiritual impulses— or as authentic as any one of us can be in this world. But the restraint that Hansen's narrator shows in revealing Mariette, prohibits any kind of single interpretation. Even at the end of the novel, are Mariette's sudden pains in a store, or with her French student, studied art, attempts to create and revel in a role? Or are they authentic spiritual signs that suggest the presence of Christ's love? Does she herself know the answer to this question? Perhaps Hansen asks us, Does it matter which answer is true, in terms of the way that Mariette herself lives?

It may be that Mariette's wounds and ecstasies are fraudulent; it may be that they are real; it may be some combination of the two.

But whatever the case, Mariette is a broken vessel that God uses anyway. Perhaps, Hansen suggests, saintliness is not about the quality of the person or the responses of the community around that person. Perhaps saintliness is about observing a quality of openness to the miraculous, an acceptance of God's evident hand. As she leaves, Mariette praises the sisters: "You let God use you" (175). Perhaps this is what defines the saintliness for which Mariette had prayed when she first came to the convent.

At the end of the novel, more than thirty years have passed since these events, and Sister Philomène, who had questioned the sensuousness of Mariette's spiritual life, is now the Reverend Mother and still in contact with Mariette, who has tended her father to his death and who now lives alone, the subject of stories and gossip. Although removed from the community, Mariette has continued to follow the liturgically oriented pattern of life of the Sisters of the Crucifixion. But the conclusion to the novel is Mariette's affirmation that the spiritual life was not meant to be completely ordered, completely patterned, completely predictable. Christ is wilder than that, she suggests in a letter to Mother Philomène, and Christ's refusal to do the expected is an encouragement to our own spiritual growth, which is accomplished not only within the context of Christ's strict ordinances, but also in the context of Christ's love: "We try to be formed and held and kept by him, but instead he offers us freedom. And now when I try to know his will, his kindness floods me, his great love overwhelms me, and I hear him whisper, Surprise me" (179). But how are readers to understand this call to surprise? What might it mean to surprise God? Is it possible to surprise an omniscient God? Is Christ, in calling for this, asking Mariette to do the impossible?

Perhaps surprise is one of the only gifts that God can give that he himself cannot have. If so, then the novel poses another question about surprise: Are we prepared, Hansen asks the reader, for Christ's surprises, surprises that will comfort and discomfort us? Are we ready for God's inexplicable character to shatter all of our order and discipline, and for the fearful ways in which he might do this? And do we realize that God may do this shattering within the context of the mundane details of our immediate world, and that the mundane and the exceptional, the concrete and the spiritual, the common and the extraordinary—that all of these come from the same God?

▓ Discussion Questions about the Novel

1. When Mariette first comes to the convent, Sister Hermance tells her that she has been praying for "consumption and an early death" (19), which seems to be the prayer of someone who has read too many romantic novels and saints' lives. When she asks Mariette what she has prayed for, Mariette replies, "I have been praying to be a great saint" (19). How are we to understand this prayer? Is it merely prideful, as Sister Hermance suggests? How are we to understand this in the context of her later prayer for humility (27)?

2. During Mariette's first interview with Mother Céline, her biological sister, Mother Céline insists, "We aren't meant to pine away and die here. We're meant to live in the heartening fullness of God" (30). In what ways do the sisters live in the "heartening fullness of God"? Is there evidence of such fullness? Is such fullness possible in the real world? If not, then isn't trying for it a vain and presumptuous thing?

3. In crafting his portrait of the Sisters of the Crucifixion, Hansen portrays a religious environment that, in its order and

rigor, seems in some ways to be ill-suited for the miraculous. How are we to evaluate this environment? Is such a context an important safeguard against spiritual excess? Or might such an environment hinder valid and perhaps even ecstatic spiritual expression? Is it possible to strike a balance between the two?

4. While Mariette's spirituality is expressed in very physical, even erotic terms, much of the spirituality shown by the sisters is expressed in ways that punish the body. Do these punishments represent a disdain for the body, a scorn for the things of the flesh? Or do these punishments represent more of an intentional mystical participation in the suffering of Christ? Are these responses inconsistent? Does suffering have spiritual value?

5. Mariette is spoken of several times as an excellent performer, and at times this is used as praise, at times as rebuke, at times as a warning. Is performance the antithesis of authentic experience? If Mariette is indeed performing, does this negate a genuine searching for God?

6. After hearing of Julian of Norwich, Mariette pens a letter in which she writes, "Christ has told me that soon he will put my faith to the proof and find out whether I truly love him and whether the offering of my heart which I so often have made to him is authentic" (43). How do you understand this claim? Is this something that Mariette longs for? If so, why? Is it problematic that Mariette is adopting spiritual motives and manifestations that Julian had expressed, manifestations that she wishes to apply to her own spiritual life? Does this remove the possibility that they are authentic?

7. Of the stigmata, Père Marriott tells Mariette, "I don't believe it's possible. I do believe it happened" (130). What might this seemingly contradictory response say about Père Marriott's spiritual life? Might his response simply be interpreted as an act of faith, a claim that though the miraculous is impossible, it breaks into this world of ours? Or is something else at stake here for Père Marriott?

8. In the end, how are we as readers to respond to the appearance of the stigmata? In a 1998 essay entitled "Stigmata," published in *Image: A Journal of the Arts and Religion*, Ron Hansen wrote that the stigmata is given to remind us: "If the fruits of stigmata are truly the esteem of the pious, the humiliation for the favored one, and hollow talk, confusion, hate, and envy, one may indeed wonder why God would grace the world with them. I do have some possible reasons for it. We are so far away from the Jesus of history that he can seem a fiction, a myth, the greatest story ever told, but no more. We have a hint of his reality, and the shame and agony of his Crucifixion, in those whom God has graced with stigmata. . . . Cynics may find in stigmata only wish fulfillment, illness, or fakery, but the faithful ought to find in them vibrant and disturbing symbols of Christ's incarnation and his painful, redemptive death on the Cross." Do you find Hansen's reasons for stigmata compelling?

▦ Other Books to Consider

—Georges Bernanos, *Diary of a Country Priest*. Translated by Pamela Morris. New York: Macmillan, 1936.

> A young, dedicated, and devout priest tenderly cares for his French parish, encountering ills, petty and large, among the parishioners to whom he is dedicated, even when those ills become vindictive.

—Willa Cather, *Death Comes for the Archbishop*. New York: Knopf, 1927.

> Two devout French priests work toward reinvigorating and establishing the Catholic church in the newly opened territory of New Mexico, where they encounter forces, natural and human, that resist them aggressively.

—Louise Erdrich, *The Last Report on the Miracles at Little No Horse*. New York: HarperCollins, 2001.

> When Father Jude comes to investigate reports of miracles associated with Sister Leopolda, a Puyat woman, in order to consider her for canonization, he is confronted with the evasiveness of Father Damien (a woman who has spent much of her life disguised as a priest), who knows through the sanctity of the confessional much about the truth of Sister Leopolda.

—Graham Greene, *The Power and the Glory*. New York: Viking Press, 1940.

> A priest, beset by alcoholism as well as an intense sense of his own failures in his faith and duties, seeks a courageous redemption through facing the possibility of his own martyrdom.

—James McBride, *Miracle at St. Anna*. New York: Riverhead Books, 2002.

> Based on a true incident during the occupation of Italy, this story of four American soldiers and the villagers with whom they take refuge speaks to an openness to the miraculous within our everyday lives.

—Mark Salzman, *Lying Awake*. New York: Knopf, 2000.

> A nun confronts the possibility that the mystical visions she has enjoyed may be, in the end, only a symptom of the epilepsy with which she has been diagnosed.

THE CHILDREN OF MEN P.D. James
(1992)

Synopsis

It is the year 2021, and the world has not seen a human birth for twenty-five years. England is ruled by Xan Lyppiat, a dictator who manages to maintain the famous British calm by providing the people with comfort, security, and pleasure. The dark underside of this world is represented by brutal penal colonies, a government-sanctioned practice of mass suicide by the elderly, and draconian immigration policies. Oxford history professor Theo Faron chronicles these events in his journal. Because he is cousin to the Warden of England and therefore has access to the reins of power, Theo is contacted by a small group of dissidents who want to protest the abuses of the government. Theo reluctantly agrees to talk to his cousin Xan, but, as he predicted, his words have little effect. Theo awaits the end of civilization and tries to forget about the dissidents, especially one young woman, Julian.

However, some time later the group contacts him again, this time with shocking news. Julian is pregnant and does not want to fall under the control of Xan and his government. Theo joins the dissidents as they cross the English countryside, now turned into wilderness, in search of a safe place for Julian to have her baby. One by one, each member of the group is hunted down and killed until only Theo stands between Julian and her newborn, and Xan and the government officials. In the final showdown, Theo comes to a deep realization of both the power of love and the love of power.

Born in 1920 in Oxford, a child of civil servants, P.D. James grew up to be a civil servant herself, working for the National Health Service and the forensics and criminal justice departments of Great Britain's Home Office until her retirement in 1979. She has also been a magistrate and a governor of the BBC. But she is best known internationally for her detective fiction. Her first novel, *Cover Her Face* (1962), marked the debut of her poet-detective Commander Adam Dalgliesh. Since then she has authored nineteen other mysteries, including *Unnatural Causes* (1967), *Shroud for a Nightingale* (1971), *Innocent Blood* (1980), *The Skull Beneath the Skin* (1982), *A Taste for Death* (1986), *Death in Holy Orders* (2001), and *The Lighthouse* (2005). To this detective fiction James has added the nonfiction account of the nineteenth-century Ratcliffe Highway murders, *The Maul and the Pear Tree* with T.A. Critchely (1971); an autobiography, *Time to Be in Earnest* (2000); and the dystopian novel, *The Children of Men*. Her work has made her into one of the premier writers of detective fiction and established the figure of Adam Dalgliesh as an icon of the genre.

James has received many honors, including the title Baroness James of Holland Park (1991). In addition, most of her novels have been adapted for television, and *Children of Men* was made into a major motion picture in 2006. While the movie retains the basic premise of a childless society, the story has been so altered as to make it almost unrecognizable to a reader of the novel.

Considering the Novel

What would happen if the world had no future, if there was no hope for a next generation, if everything that exists now was doomed to crumble and fade away with no one to bear witness? This is the world P.D. James imagines in *The Children of Men*. In James's dystopian vision, the last human beings, the Omega generation, have been born twenty-five years earlier and the whole human race is simply waiting to become extinct. James says that her inspiration for the novel came from reading a report on the dramatic and unexplained drop in the fertility rate in the Western world. Perhaps, too, James was inspired by contemporary Western society's incessant focus on the present moment. In this novel, such a focus is taken to a logical though ironic extreme: there is no future, only the immediate present. There is nothing to hope for, since within a generation, there will be no witness. There is only surviving the moment, for tomorrow we die, and there are none to come after. Thus the first half of the novel, titled "Omega" after the final letter in the Greek alphabet, describes a world that has lost its goal, its *telos,* and has been overcome by spiritual torpor.

Much of our knowledge of this doomed world comes through entries in the journal of an Oxford professor of history, Theo Faron. On New Year's Day 2021, Theo begins to write as "one small defence against personal accidie" (3), but the tone of his writings is not so much a defense against as a reflection of his own despair. Theo is not a great storyteller; his style is epigrammatic, just bordering on cliché. While we are intrigued by the idea of what this world without a future is like, we may at the same time be put off by the tone of the novel, of Theo's journal. The voice is cold, sterile, stripped down.

Theo's descriptions of his life, his family, and his actions do not inspire empathy in the reader. Instead, he appears to take pains to establish himself as someone with no connections to the world around him, jaded about his past, and coldly realistic about the future. The cynical words of his diary appear designed to help Theo break with a past that is painful to him. He is brutal in describing his parents and his child. Even his relationship to his old college mentor is submitted to withering scorn. Perhaps his snide words and remarks are just a way to neutralize the hurt he feels. Or perhaps Theo is really just a lonely, embittered man waiting out the time until his death and the death of the human race.

Theo's chronicle of his childhood and marriage are indeed disturbing. Instead of the warm nostalgia we might expect of a memoir, he describes growing up in "an atmosphere redolent of resentment" (14). A mother consumed by petty jealousies and a distant dying father helped to shape Theo into the adult he has become. Theo's memories of his father are clouded by images and smells of death and disease. He says, "For months after his death I was visited by a recurrent nightmare in which I would see him at the foot of my bed pointing at me a bleeding yellow stump, not of a finger but of a whole hand. . . . [N]ow he never comes. I am glad that he has finally gone, taking with him his pain, his blood, his pus. But I wish that he had left me a different memory" (27). This horrific image is told in a cold and detached tone, yet the final sentence sounds a plaintive note. We wonder again about who Theo really is and what his motivations in writing this memoir might be.

Theo also states quite baldly that he killed his daughter. The declaration seems intended to shock, but since the diary is meant for no eyes but his own, whom is he intending to shock? He goes on to soften his declaration, explaining that her death was due to an accident—but then he drops yet another bombshell. He admits that although he did love his child he "would have felt more had she been prettier . . . more affectionate, more responsive, less inclined to whine" (29). He recognizes that "[s]he has been dead for almost twenty-seven years and I still think of her with complaint" (29). Is this ruthless honesty about himself or complete self-centeredness? And even if his negative view of himself and those around him may be characterized as brutal honesty, why is it so difficult to feel empathy for Theo?

Our view of Theo's misanthropy is confirmed when he goes to visit his old college mentor, an irascible man whom Theo admits has treated him generously over the years. When Jasper suggests that he might move into Theo's overlarge house in Oxford, Theo is horrified. The thought of sharing his home with another person, particularly one who might need his care, is abhorrent to Theo. And while this might be understandable, Theo's complete lack of gratitude toward the professor, as well as his mocking descriptions of the man, once again do little to endear him to the reader.

It is hard to feel sympathy for a man who admits so little love for his fellow human beings, yet at the same time, his unflinching self-assessment and honesty are oddly admirable—and perhaps both are qualities necessary to survive given the new reality that the human race must face extinction. In a society where everyone seems to do all they can to avoid pain and discomfort, Theo is willing to turn a cold, clinical eye on himself and on what is happening around him and to assess it honestly. While he may not have hope for the future, he has not allowed himself to be blinded to the reality of the situation around him.

As Theo describes his world, we feel troubling jolts of recognition. Many of the problems faced in this brave, new world are exaggerations of, or perhaps the logical extension of, issues that confront us now. Our current problems of apathy and ignorance, of a blind trust in the power of science and technology, of religion pandering to the public, have been magnified in James's vision of the world.

England in the year 2021, as Theo describes it, remains the last bastion of civilization, still a democracy in name, but in reality ruled as a dictatorship by a Warden (Theo's cousin Xan) and his Council of four advisors. Theo notes wryly that most citizens don't bother to vote, can't be bothered to sit on a jury, and seem content to stand by silently as their rights are curtailed and power is increasingly centralized. As he explains, "The system has the merit of simplicity and gives the illusion of democracy to people who no longer have the energy to care how or by whom they are governed as long as they get what the Warden has promised: freedom from fear, freedom from want, freedom from boredom" (89). As voter participation rates go down in Western societies and as freedoms we have assumed for generations seem threatened, is James trying to warn us that we may also be lulled into complacency by laziness and the need to avoid boredom, and so are seduced by a government that satisfies needs for us?

Other elements of this dystopian society also seem to be an amplification or distortion of troubling contemporary trends. Terms such as "Sojourners" and "The Quietus" point to present-day troubling controversies over immigration and euthanasia. Sojourners are healthy, strong immigrants who are imported to England to perform labor that the English cannot or will not do: clean the sewers, care for the elderly. They are welcomed in when they are young and useful, but forcibly deported when they are old and may require aid from the state they have served. The Quietus, the mass suicide of the old, begins as a voluntary, sanitary way for society to facilitate the death wishes of incapacitated elderly. Yet when Theo witnesses a Quietus, it is clear that not all the participants are volunteers. Are a poetic label and a romantic ritual all that are needed to keep society from questioning the justice or morality of such a practice?

But Theo, like most of British society, is resigned to the fate of the world. He doesn't ask about the causes of the epidemic of infertility nor does he expect a cure. Instead he comments matter-of-factly on how the world has reacted to the betrayal—to the death—of its gods. When first confronted with an epidemic of infertility, the world trusted confidently in the power of Western science, just as today we trust that problems of global warming, AIDS, or diminishing energy sources will be solved through science. We feel, along with citizens in Theo's world, that Western science "has preserved, comforted, healed, warmed, fed and entertained us and we have felt free to criticize and occasionally reject it as men have always rejected their gods, but in the knowledge that, despite our apostasy, this deity, our creature and our slave, would still provide for us; the anaesthetic for the pain, the spare heart, the new lung, the antibiotic, the moving wheels and the moving pictures" (5). But in the world of James's novel, it has become clear that the gods of science and technology cannot save the world—a devastating blow to the collective Western ego. Theo acknowledges that "we are humiliated at the very heart of our faith in ourselves" (6).

When technology fails, humanity turns to a more transcendent God. But religion does not seem to offer any adequate solutions either. Theo tells the reader that the hellfire and brimstone preachers who arose shortly after the Omega year soon gave way to a new sort of theology preached by one Rosie McClure. Rosie preaches a soothing gospel of love which demands nothing of its adherents and promises them a heaven that is "an eternal Costa del Sol liberally supplied with food, drink, sun and sexual pleasure" (49). At the opposite extreme are the flagellants who inhabit the public parks, seeking to appease an angry God. The Anglican Church, much beloved by James, has also fallen prey to the degradation that characterizes so much of society. The priests have stooped to baptizing kittens as nostalgic replacements for the human infants who no longer exist, and the church has "moved from the theology of sin and redemption to a less uncompromising doctrine: corporate social responsibility coupled with a sentimental humanism" (50). And in the face of global disaster, some muse angrily that perhaps mankind is simply God's failed experiment: "Perhaps He's just baffled. Seeing the mess, not knowing how to put it right. Perhaps not wanting to put it right. Perhaps He only had enough power left for one final intervention. So He made it. Whoever He is, whatever He is, I hope He burns in His own hell" (90–91).

Theo's unhappy but placid life is disturbed when Julian, a former student, asks him to use his influence with his cousin, the Warden of England. Julian belongs to a small band of dissidents who advocate for changes in some of the more egregious government practices. Theo, although convinced that his meeting with Xan will change nothing, agrees to go, primarily because something in Julian has touched him. Julian and one other member of her group are professing Christians; they believe passionately that the goals of the council should be "[c]ompassion, justice, love" (60). Although Theo confronts them with the inescapable fact that society does not, in fact, care about those things but instead wants only "protection, comfort, and pleasure," something about them touches him. Cold, clear-eyed Theo may actually still have within him a spark of hope. Yet in the end, the cynical, practical Theo appears to be right: his meeting with Xan changes nothing except to make Xan aware that there is a group agitating against his policies.

Part I ends at a stalemate. The revolutionaries, "the Five Fishes," publish a tract laying out their beliefs. Although the State Security Police investigates the revolutionaries and Theo, nothing more seems to come of the investigation. Theo resolves to put the matter behind him and sets out on a sort of farewell tour, once again resigned to the inevitable end of the world as he knows it. The issues have been raised, the characters have been laid out; we have only to see what will become of this sad, dying society.

Part II begins six months later and its title, "Alpha" signals a new beginning. The voice and tone of the second half of the book is distinctly different from the first. Because Theo no longer writes in his journal, the pace of the story quickens and the amount of dialogue increases. Reflections on societal problems give way to action and suspense. Instead of a meditation on what happens to a society that has no hope, the novel seems to become pure adventure story. The contrast between the two parts is sharp and leads the reader to wonder what to make of such changes. Some may find the second part more creative, more interesting. Or perhaps it becomes too unbelievable: Theo converted into an action-movie hero, gangs of youths with painted faces attacking and ritualistically killing their victims accompanied by war whoops and tribal dancing, a gun battle between the dictator and the hero.

At the same time, the musings on the meaning and purpose of life of the first part give way to obvious Christian symbolism. Indeed, James has said that while she set out to write a dystopian novel, what she ended up with was a Christian fable. (A lifelong member of the Church of England, James has said that she never seems to write a book that doesn't have a practicing Christian in it.)

Now as the novel continues to narrate a tale of a fallen future world, it draws its structure, its characters, and its imagery from a story we know very well: the birth of Jesus. The Alpha, the new beginning, presents us with all the elements of the Nativity story. Julian is pregnant—the first expectant woman in twenty-five years—and afraid of what the Warden and Council will do to her and the child. She flees far from her home into the countryside accompanied by her husband, a priest, a midwife, and Theo, the history professor. Theo wonders, "Could ever aims and means have been so mismatched? Had there ever been an enterprise of such immense importance embarked upon by such frail and pathetically inadequate adventurers?" (158). The answer, of course, is "yes." James has taken the Nativity story and recast it more than 2,000 years into the future. As readers, we are jolted out of a futuristic mind frame to reconsider issues brought to the fore through allusion to the age-old story of hope and redemption.

The religious imagery and themes of sacrifice and betrayal build throughout the second part of the novel. The characters' names take on added significance as fault lines are drawn. Theo, Luke, and Miriam are on the side of good and try to help Julian, whose name recalls the fourteenth-century mystic Julian of Norwich, who despite suffering insisted on the goodness and love of God. Rolf, whose name means wolf, becomes a Judas figure once he decides to betray the group when he learns that he is not the father of Julian's child. When the group is attacked by a group of Omegas, Luke chooses to draw their attention to him, offering his own life to save that of Julian and the unborn child. When Julian later comments on Luke's sacrifice, Miriam recognizes, "He died to save all of us" (186).

Finally, Julian has her baby in a dilapidated woodshed in the middle of nowhere. Theo, having declared his love for Julian, has taken the position of Joseph as the surrogate father of the child. Xan and his council are desperately hunting the group, although unlike the biblical King Herod, Xan wants to appropriate the child as his own rather than kill him. When the four members of the council at last arrive, three of them occupy the position of the magi while the fourth is identified with Simeon, pronouncing his "Nunc Dimittis." The image James has drawn brings to mind a lovely renaissance nativity painting, one exuding peace and hope.

But although we've followed the parallel tracks of the Nativity story and of Julian and her baby, something is not quite right. While Joseph fled from the tyrant Herod, Theo now has blood on his hands. In order to protect Julian and her baby, Theo has killed his cousin Xan. Furthermore, he has taken Xan's ring—the ring that symbolizes ultimate power—and put it on his own finger. While on the one hand there is hope in the fact that Theo has finally overcome the ennui that gripped him in the first part of the novel, on the other hand, we cannot help but be disturbed. For all the transcendent imagery in these final scenes, the birth of this child may not bring salvation to the human race. Although it appears that the human race will survive, this child is not a messiah. Life simply goes on, much as it has before. "So it begins again. Theo thought, it begins again, with jealousy, with treachery, with violence, with murder, with this ring on my finger" (240).

Although the novel leaves us with the question of whether Theo will become a dictator like his cousin, it also leaves us with hope. Theo, a jaded, confirmed unbeliever, has been changed because of his contact with Julian, a deeply Christian woman. Even though he has trouble reconciling what he believes to be true about the world with Julian's trust in God, he has been changed by his contact with her. He has been rejuvenated; he is now able to love sacrificially.

> He contemplated the gulf fixed between Julian and himself by her belief, but without dismay. He could not diminish it but he could stretch his hands across it. And perhaps in the end the bridge would be love. . . . He could only wish her good. He would put her good before his own. He could no longer separate himself from her. He would die for her life. (226–27)

The novel ends with Theo christening the baby, and the final words are "the sign of the cross." Perhaps there is hope for this world after all.

In the end, what are we to make of this novel? Is it a warning that science and technology will fail us? Is it a lament for the loss of so many things that James sees as markers of civilization: the university, the traditional family, the Anglican Church and its liturgy? Is it a cautionary tale about the ultimate end of so many current policies and societal trends? Perhaps, fifteen years after the novel was first published, we have become immune to the losses James feared while she was writing. Has Western culture become bored and lulled by a desire to have someone care for us, to provide security and entertainment? Or perhaps the losses have not been as great as James supposed. Maybe we, too, have been able to continue on, to find hope in the future. As James herself admitted, she was unable to write a completely dystopian novel; she had to end on a note of hope.

And that may be the best way to read this book.

■ Discussion Questions about the Novel

1. In her autobiography, *Time to be in Earnest* (1999), James has written that "[e]ven as a child I had a sense that I was two people; the one who experienced the trauma, the pain, the happiness, and the other who stood aside and watched with a disinterested ironic eye" (67). To what extent do you see James the author embodied in the character of Theo? Do we need such outside observers in order to see the world more clearly? Or does this cold, distant eye distort the truth?

2. Although this is a futuristic novel, it is not at all technological. Does the absence of science fiction details weaken the novel or make it more believable?

3. At the end of the novel, Julian is the only member of the Five Fishes still alive and Theo is wearing the Warden's ring. How do you imagine the world under his rule?

4. The reading public did not take to this novel as it had taken to James's detective fiction. (It has never sold very well.) However, this is also the novel by James that has generated the most discussion and controversy in theological circles. Does it work as a novel? Are you drawn into the story? Or does it seem to be more of a theological essay in story form?

5. At the beginning of the novel, Theo seems determined to stay out of the mainstream of society. He has resigned from the council and leads a fairly solitary existence. Yet he responds almost immediately to Julian and does everything she asks. Why? Is it a case of libido, and is James drawing too heavily on gender stereotypes? Or is Theo genuinely looking for redemption? Is he trying to make up for the death of his daughter by helping to bring a new life into the world?

6. Some readers have said that this is a book about aging and dying, infused with nostalgia and perhaps remorse. Does such a personal perspective on the novel take away from its social critique? Or does it add another layer of richness?

7. James harshly judges the religious practices of the church in the final days of the world. What, in your view, should be the positive role of the church in such end times? Does James imply some sort of answer?

■ Other Books to Consider

—Cormac McCarthy, *The Road*. New York: Random House, 2006.

> In another postapocalyptic landscape, a father and son struggle to stay alive in a world that seems to have died, finding within their relationship a hope for "goodness."

—George Orwell, *Nineteen Eighty-Four*. New York: Harcourt, Brace, 1947.

> In this classic dystopian novel, Winston Smith—along with all his fellow citizens—is trapped in a totalitarian society, his every move catalogued and constricted by "Big Brother." Although his subversive efforts are ultimately ineffective, he regains, at least in part, a sense of his own human spirit.

—John Steinbeck, *The Winter of Our Discontent*. New York: Viking, 1961.

> Steinbeck's devastating critique of easy and complacent middle class America puts Ethan Allen Hawley on stage. His story begins on Good Friday, 1960, with Hawley as a store clerk with a restless wife and unhappy children, and leads to his awful realization that he can be lulled into the shady morality that marks his own petty world.

—John Updike, *Toward the End of Time*. New York: Knopf, 1997.

> It is the year 2020, and a war between China and the United States has devastated the population, resulting in social chaos. Ben Turnbull, like Theo, negotiates the new realities of his world and tries to work his own way toward a future that seems to be marked only by extinction.

THE SPARROW and
(1996)

THE CHILDREN
OF GOD   Mary Doria Russell
(1998)

Mary Doria Russell's science fiction debut, *The Sparrow*, and its sequel, *The Children of God*—twin halves of a single long story—follow the career of Emilio Sandoz, a Jesuit priest who is sent to Alpha Centuri in 2019 after a satellite picks up the sound of beautiful music emanating from that planetary system. Sandoz, a brilliant linguist in love with God but prone to doubt, willingly sets off to the planet Rahkat in company with a group of lively, likable explorers who banter about God's benevolence, humor, and sovereignty as they journey to this new world.

Forty years later, Sandoz returns—or *is returned*—to Earth, a bitter, broken, and disgraced man. His friends are dead, his hands are mutilated, his health is precarious, and his soul and will are nearly destroyed. The entire world knows him only as a murderer and a prostitute. His earthly family, the Jesuits, protect him from the outside world and himself. They struggle to heal his body, his mind, and his soul, but his scars are deep. *The Sparrow* teases out the story of Sandoz's life during the forty years between 2019 and 2059—the initial joys of the exploring party, the sense that God had truly called them to their work, and then the loss of everything— friendship, liberty, faith, life itself.

In *The Children of God*, Sandoz is forcibly sent back to Rahkat by the Father General of the Jesuits to work out his spiritual restoration. Unknown to anyone on Earth, during Sandoz's absence the culture on Rahkat has undergone a radical transformation, sparked by the changes initiated by members of the initial exploratory party. The lower class Runa, outnumbering the ruling Jana'ata ten to one, are massacring their former oppressors. Sofia, Sandoz's dear friend marooned on Rahkat, is leading a ruthless Runa hoard, believing herself to be a freedom fighter. Meanwhile, small bands of Runa and Jana'ata, escaping the madness and turmoil that have engulfed their world, form communities that eventually coalesce into an egalitarian society.

In this complex revolutionary context, Sandoz seeks answers to his spiritual questions—and he finds them as, against all instinct, he champions the cause of the Jana'ata and so becomes the savior of the species that abused him. Through this act and the kindness and love of others, he begins to understand once again the joys and realities of religious faith and the place of risk in making the leap toward belief.

On the Author

Born near Chicago in 1950, Mary Doria Russell pursued an academic career in social, cultural, and biological anthropology. She later taught human gross anatomy at Case Western Reserve University for much of the 1980s, writing on cannibalism, craniofacial biomechanics, bone biology, and nuclear magnetic resonance scanners. She ultimately left academia to write fiction. Born and raised a Catholic, Russell has converted to Judaism, though she maintains strong connections to her Catholic education. Her religious explorations have had a strong impact on her writing, particularly in her willingness to ask difficult, heartrending questions about God's faithfulness and love.

■ Considering the Novel

When Father Sandoz returns from Rahket after his first mission, he has been destroyed physically and, more devastatingly, spiritually. He went to Rahkat because he was called by God to go. He traveled across a lifetime to be a witness for God, and to respond to the beauty that had called him across a galaxy. He was, he believed, completely in God's hands. And it seemed, for a time, that everything about the mission affirmed this clear sense of vocation. But in the end, the first mission leads to disaster on many levels—including the death of most of the crew, the destruction of Runa communities, and the plunging of Father Sandoz into forced prostitution. When it seems that only despair is left, Father Sandoz lashes out—and unexpectedly kills the child that had befriended him, and who had come to save him—suggesting to Sandoz that God, in allowing this to occur, could only be perceived as malicious. "I loved God and trusted in His love. . . . I had nothing between me and what happened but the love of God. And I was raped" (*Children of God*, 4–5), he complains—and is seemingly justified.

Emilio Sandoz's accusation against God captures the essence of Russell's examination of the risks associated with religious faith. How do we know that our faith is leading us in the right paths? Is it possible that God will not be faithful? Can faith in an almighty God leave the believer vulnerable and exposed? Since we are mortal and our scope is limited, can our faith be meaningful, when we are denied its larger significance and results?

The faithful have categories into which they may place God and his actions, but God has not agreed to be constrained by these categories, Russell suggests. The faithful trust that God is love, but love can cause incalculable pain. Traveling to Rahkat the first time, Sandoz is eager to make first contact with a new world, and he is sure—he *knows*—that God is calling him to this mission. Yet he confides to his associate Anne his fear of fully loving God: "You know what's the most terrifying thing about admitting that you're in love? You are just naked. The only thing that makes it tolerable is to believe the other person loves you back and that you can trust him not to hurt you" (*Sparrow*, 179). But when people of faith are hurt, their suffering can lead them to this exceptionally painful question: has God caused the suffering? To even entertain the idea that a loving, all powerful God can cause—or allow—suffering can be numbing. Russell's novels explore the ways that people of faith react to such dark nights of the soul.

But it is not all darkness. Belief in an all-powerful God has its rewards as well, Russell suggests. Faith also provides joy, hope, and restoration in the lives of the faithful, and so the novels are laced with signs of God's presence and goodness. Children, fidelity, solidarity among the community of believers, and a sense of God's long view of history, hint that belief is worth pain and suffering—despite the possibility of those dark nights, and despite the knowledge that we may not live to see the purposes of God fulfilled, purposes which may have been propelled or encouraged by the seeds of our faithfulness but which do not bloom within our seeing.

Sandoz's suffering is exacerbated by the violation of two convictions that initially give him joy and comfort: his vow of celibacy and his belief that the journey to Rahkat is the will of God. Sandoz's celibacy is a recurring motif that illustrates both the risks and joys of religious life. Though Sandoz does eventually renounce his vows, Russell portrays his single-minded devotion to God as a beautiful and reasonable commitment. When trying to explain his celibacy, he says that he is "free to love without exclusion, and to serve many" (*Children of God*, 51). When Sandoz must decide between God and Sofia, the woman he loves, he ponders that it is time "to weigh the extraordinary and spiritual and fathomless beauty that God had shown him against the ordinary and worldly and incalculable sweetness of human love and family" (*Sparrow*, 306). Sandoz's vow and his fidelity to God seem to be confirmed when on his knees he believes "with all his heart . . . that his love affair with God has been consummated" (*Sparrow*, 189). Celibacy has provided Sandoz with unspeakable comfort and joy, because it has offered him a deep relationship with God which is here fulfilled.

But this willful vulnerability has also left him defenseless. Sandoz risks all, believing that what he is doing is God's will. When God apparently does not uphold his side of the bargain—in fact, when Sandoz is abandoned to the worst sexual debauchery, which mocks his celibacy—and when even his rescue is turned to irony and ashes, Sandoz is devastated. So, having been abandoned by God, he rejects his obedience and faith in a God of malice.

Belief in an all-powerful God brings with it the comfort that God controls history and that ordinary human events are held within the will of God. Sandoz and his companions feel this certainty while traveling to Rahkat the first time. The signs seem to be there. The signs *are* there. The Jesuits easily organize and fund the mission. The long and dangerous voyage through space is uneventful. The welcome they receive is overwhelming. Rahkat itself has an edenic appearance. Thoughts of the risks associated with faith are far from anyone's mind. Sandoz sees the unfolding of God's will, and he himself is playing a key role in that unfolding. He is in God's hand.

But Sandoz's dark night comes quickly and brutally. One by one, his companions waste away and die or are murdered. Caught up in the Runa revolt, Sandoz is captured by the Jana'ata and sentenced to die. Given sanctuary by Supaari, a Jana'ata merchant, he submits to hasta'akala, a procedure that renders his hands as useless as ivy hanging from a tree. The procedure saves him from execution, but his independence vanishes and he must rely on the good graces of foreigners. Hope is ignited in his soul when Supaari sends him to Hlavin Kitheri, Reshtar of Inbrokar—the musician who created the beautiful music that drew them to Rahkat. Sandoz, still believing and trusting that God leads, speculates that "I have been brought here, step by step, to meet this man: Hlavin Kitheri, a poet—perhaps even a prophet—who of all his kind might know the God whom I serve" (*Sparrow*, 390). Instead Kitheri rapes him, passes him to his courtiers, and is inspired to create beautiful poems and music based on this debauchery—the ironically awful inspiration for the music the party has heard.

Eventually, Sandoz is left in a cell to await his next rapist, and to ponder his utter isolation and God's abandonment. Resolving to escape when his cell door next opens, he mistakenly kills the gentle Askama, a Runa child and his dearest companion, in the presence of his earthling rescuers. His return to earth is preceded by his infamous reputation: the world community has already rendered judgment. In good faith, Sandoz risked all for the glory of God; now, his life and soul hang in the balance.

In *The Sparrow*, Russell sympathizes with Sandoz's suffering and his anger toward God, giving him time to grieve and ponder the value of loving God. His Jesuit family has nearly unlimited patience and forbearance in spite of public opinion and the financial burden of caring for him; the loving Christian community of believers sustains and nurtures Sandoz when he has lost everything. With the possible exception of Johannes Voelker, every Jesuit refutes Sandoz's accusations against himself and against God through word or deed. The Father General treats him as a beloved son. Ed Behr and John Candotti faithfully attend to his physical and emotional needs. But *The Sparrow* ends with a disturbing question: can God's silence—or inexplicability—be so devastating that one loses faith itself?

In *The Children of God,* Russell prods Sandoz to move on. Anger is cathartic, but he is pushed to overcome his anger and to regain his joy. Thus Sandoz's companions on the *Giordano Bruno,* the second vessel, teach Sandoz to live with the tension of belief both in an omnipotent, inscrutable God and in unspeakable evil. Their relationships are much more adversarial than in *The Sparrow,* because Sandoz is in need of confrontation. Sean Fein offers him this pragmatic advice: "Pucker up and kiss the cross. Make all this mean something. Redeem it" (*Children of God,* 268). Indeed, perseverance in the face of numerous disasters is an enduring characteristic of Sandoz, the very quality that leads the Father General to send him back to Rakhat so that he might once again find God: "It became more apparent to the Father General that Sandoz was truly called to walk this strange and difficult, this unnatural and unutterable path to God, which required not poetry or piety but simple endurance and patience" (*Sparrow,* 160). On Rakhat for the second time, Sandoz clings to the hope that there must be answers other than the one that declares that God is cruel. Though the answers come with painful slowness, he does not give up. As he confides to his friend John Candotti, "I keep thinking of that line: if you are asked to go a mile, go two. Maybe this is the extra mile. Maybe I've got to give it all another chance. I can tolerate a great deal if I just understand why. . . . And there's only one place I can find that out" (*Children of God,* 289).

If there were only risks associated with religious faith, religion would fade away. But while there are few answers, and suffering and darkness are widespread, evidence of God's love and faithfulness are present as well. The love of Gina brings Sandoz back from the brink of destruction. Human touch and affection are intoxicating to a man so long without either; we almost hear and see vitality, warmth, and laughter seeping back into Sandoz's body and mind as he falls in love with Gina. He begins to take care of himself, to exercise and to eat well. It is difficult to reconcile the strength of Sandoz's convictions regarding celibacy during the first trip and his desire for Gina during his rehabilitation, but it is significant that Sandoz is able to love again. He is again able to be vulnerable, to trust that Gina will not hurt him. Russell suggests that one way back to loving God may be through human love.

Sandoz's dogged search for answers runs up against the inscrutable nature of God—who is, paradoxically, both the central and the most obscure character in these novels. Russell wants to show that believers may seek God earnestly, but that he can be frustratingly difficult to find. Thus the novels are filled with uncertainty: characters long for a clear declaration of God's intentions. Yet there are no easy answers from God in life, and Russell doesn't allow any in these novels. "Have you ever wondered about the story of Cain?" Sandoz askes Ed Behr, a close Jesuit companion. "He made his sacrifice in good faith. Why did God refuse it?" (*Sparrow*, 285). When Sandoz struggles with his decision to love Sofia or to remain celibate, Russell's narrator comments dryly that "God was silent on the matter" (*Sparrow*, 307). Sean, Sandoz's outspoken Irish-Jewish companion, while discussing the extinction of the Jana'ata with Lady Suukmel, declares that "there's just no telling whom God will take a liking to" (*Children of God*, 363). Ariana, Sandoz's daughter, after recounting the death of Gina, admits, "God never explains" (*Children of God*, 436). Squaring an all-powerful loving God with evil is difficult, Russell affirms, but confronting a God who is not eager to reveal answers makes the task of reconciliation even harder for Sandoz.

There comes a point in Sandoz's life when he understands that he is both an observer of, and participant in, God's long view of history. At that point, his personal suffering becomes, in his mind, less important than God's plan. Belief in an all-powerful God allows the faithful to hope that God controls history. Those around Sandoz never forget this hope, but Sandoz needs to be reminded. "Because I trust God," the Father General writes in his explanation of why he orchestrated Sandoz's second trip to Rahkat, "I trust also that you will have learned something of value on your journey" (*Children of God*, 431). The pope confidently tells Sandoz that "you will live to see what you have made possible when you return to Rahkat. God is waiting for you in the ruins" (*Children of God*, 36–37).

Sandoz begins to understand his role in God's long view of history during the second voyage to Rahkat. He becomes the savior of the species that nearly destroyed him: in a bargain reminiscent of Abraham, Sandoz asks Sofia if she will spare the Jana'ata "if I can find you ten" innocent people (*Children of God*, 412). As he observes God's hand in history, Sandoz begins to see a purpose for his suffering. While discussing the fate of the Jana'ata, Sandoz says, "I left the priesthood, Sofia, I was done with God." "But He wasn't done with you," she counters. Wearily he answers, "Evidently not" (*Children of God*, 414). Candotti suggests, "Maybe that was God's way of telling us that we can never know His intentions, but as time goes on . . . we'll understand. We'll see where He was: we'll see His back" (*Children of God*, 428). Russell here depicts the gradual path taken by many people of faith. There are seldom epiphanies and clear declarations of God's hand in events; but like Sandoz, those desperately seeking clues that affirm God's goodness and his hand in history either find them or have faith that they will. Sandoz, because of the time distortion caused by his space flights, is given a sense of that long view of history: he is witness to the new society on Rahkat, a society based on equality and not oppression, filled with a knowledge of God—with a distinctly Jewish flare.

Is Sandoz restored? Does he return to the joy and vulnerability he exhibited when he professed his fidelity to God as he first knelt on the soil of Rahkat? The reader is never quite sure of the level or intensity of his spiritual restoration. The suffering he experienced because of his religious faith will always temper and shape his future joy. The last scene in *The Children of God* takes place in a cemetery. Sandoz is confronted with three strong emotions: joy, grief, and hope. He is joyful when he discovers that he had a child with Gina. He grieves when he discovers Gina has recently died and he will never see her again. He is hopeful when he holds his grandson. Joy, grief, and hope represent the stages of Sandoz's life in these novels. Joy is difficult to sustain in a world filled with grief, but hope encourages the faithful to continue seeking the joys of a loving God.

Sandoz's response to his suffering and God's complicity is intense, but not unusual among believers. The reader is led to expect in the opening chapters of *The Sparrow* that an inquisition, albeit a benign one, into the actions of Sandoz is the object of the post-trip narrative. In reality, Sandoz turns the inquisition into an inquiry into the character of God. Sandoz is both prosecutor and witness, and he takes full advantage of his infirmities and suffering to level a charge of infidelity against God. Either God is in control of events or he is not, argues Sandoz. If God is in control, then he is cruel and unfaithful and Sandoz, at least, has "the solace of hating God." If God is not in control, Sandoz seethes, then we are simply "deluded apes" (*Children of God*, 5). These are not pleasant alternatives to contemplate, but ones with which broken people throughout Judeo-Christian history have wrestled. Many Old Testament writers questioned God's motives: Jeremiah, Ezekiel, Zachariah, David, and other psalmists asked why God was silent, why he allowed injustice, and why the wicked prosper and the righteous suffer. "O LORD, how long shall the wicked, how long shall the wicked exult?" (Psalm 94:3). The form of the question changes with the advancing centuries and with emerging theologies, but the heartbreaking question remains the same: Why does God only watch the sparrow fall? Why does he not put out his hand to save the tiny bird?

Sandoz's Jesuit training and rational, textbook theological answers are insufficient for the magnitude of his suffering. His world falls apart. "I loved God . . . and I was raped," he states with devastating simplicity. Sandoz believes that because he is doing all for the greater glory of God, God will—or should—bless his efforts. Clearly, he implies, God does not. Because of this rationalistic perspective, Sandoz is left with a troubling dichotomy: God is either cruel or helpless. Sandoz is devastated because he cannot accept either conclusion.

Are these the only conclusions Sandoz could have gleaned from his suffering? Russell eventually discards rational, academic notions of theodicy and invites the reader to reflect on other explanations of how God works in the universe. In a note included in the novels, Russell herself states that "we seem to believe that if we act in accordance with our understanding of God's will, we ought to be rewarded. But in doing so we're making a deal that God didn't sign on to. In our world, if people believe at all, they believe that God is love. God is hearts and flowers, and that God will send you theological candy all the time. But, if you read the Torah, you realize that God has a lot to answer for. God is a complex personality."

So eventually, Sandoz jettisons his rational arguments that seem to force an omnipotent God and operative evil to coexist. "In the absence of certainty," writes Russell, "faith is more than mere opinion; it is hope" (*Children of God*, 431). With that hope, we see, at the end of *The Children of God*, a man at peace. He has saved the Jana'ata from extinction. His nightmares have ended. He discovers that he has a child through his brief courtship of Gina and he holds his grandchild. In the end, Russell does not provide an answer to the problem of theodicy, other than to acknowledge it as a mystery for the faithful to wrestle with. But she holds out the potential for restoration and a life of joy.

▨ Discussion Questions about the Novel

1. The science fiction genre allows Russell to play with the notion of time, giving Sandoz the ability to participate personally in God's long view of history. Other than allowing Sandoz to be somewhat "outside of time," what was gained by setting these novels on another planet rather than simply making them historical novels?

2. From the moment of discovering that there is life beyond Earth, we as readers—and the Jesuit travelers—assume that the Rahkatians are children of God, sentient beings with souls. Yet Russell feels compelled to provide physical evidence for the harmony between humans, Runa, and Jana'ata, through Isaac's discovery of God's music in DNA. Was this physical evidence necessary? Did it complement the story or detract from it?

3. Hundreds, maybe thousands, of books have wrestled with the problem of a sovereign God and the existence of evil. What do Russell's novels contribute to this discussion? Were you satisfied with her attempt?

4. Children are minor but pervasive characters in *The Children of God*. At the darkest hour, children are born. Sofia gives birth to the autistic Isaac, discoverer of the sacred, unifying music. Ha'anala, Anne's namesake and Isaac's companion, eventually becomes a leader in the evolving Rahkatian society. The slaughter of children causes the Runa to revolt. Supaari leaves status and wealth to protect his newborn child. The Runa child, Askama, is the mediator between humans and the Runa. Celestina, Gina's precocious child, melts Sandoz's heart and is the instrument that binds him to her mother. Later, Sandoz holds his grandchild and finds "room in the crowded

necropolis of his heart" (*Children of God*, 436). In what ways
do you think children become symbolic in the novels?

5. As in Frederick Buechner's *Godric*, others see Sandoz as a
   saint even if he would scoff at the notion. All those close to
   him believe that Sandoz will find his answers and that these
   answers will draw him closer to God. D.W. Yarbrough and
   Marc Robichaux, his Jesuit companions, send transmissions
   back to Earth documenting his rapport with God. Vincent
   Giuliani, the Father General, sees Sandoz's struggle not as
   a move toward atheism but as a journey toward heightened
   awareness of God—and he, too, is sure that God is close to
   Sandoz. "He is still held fast in the formless stone," Giuliani
   laments, "but he's closer to God right now than I have ever
   been in my life. And I don't even have the courage to envy
   him" (*Sparrow*, 400). The pope declares, even after Sandoz
   rails that God is not innocent, "You are beloved of God"
   (*Children of God*, 36). Deep in his heart, and clearly seen by
   those around him, he is a saint. Would you agree?

▓ Other Books to Consider

—James Blish, *A Case of Conscience*. New York: Ballantine, 1958.

> When a team of scientists, including a Jesuit, arrive on the planet
> Lithia to evaluate its fusion materials, they are confronted with
> a gardenlike world and inhabitants with a strange biology. The
> Jesuit believes the planet provides proof of the heresy that Satan
> was the original creator. After a larval form of this life is brought
> back to Earth, this belief seems confirmed to him, leading him
> toward excommunication and genocide.

—C.S. Lewis, *A Grief Observed*. London: Faber and Faber, 1961.

> In heartrending and brutally honest expression, Lewis chronicles his own journey through the grief of his wife's death, a journey from a loss of faith and belief in God's provision toward a return to faith.

—C.S. Lewis, *Out of the Silent Planet*. London: Bodley Head, 1938.

> When Ransom, a Cambridge philologist, is abducted by Weston and Devine, two intellectual criminals, he is taken to Malacandra—the planet Mars. There, Ransom is drawn into both a strange beauty and a strange horror, which Lewis uses to explore the theological underpinnings of western society.

—C.S. Lewis, *Perelandra*. London: Bodley Head, 1943.

> In this, the second volume of Lewis's space trilogy, Ransom is brought to the planet Venus—Perelandra—where he again confronts Weston, who has brought demonic temptation to an unfallen world.

—Walter M. Miller, Jr., *A Canticle for Leibowitz*. Philadelphia: Lippincott, 1959.

> When a nuclear war devastates the globe, the remnants of humanity blame literacy for the destruction and mark books for burning. Leibowitz, a Jew converted to Catholicism, founds an order to protect books and is eventually martyred. Centuries later, the priest Francis finds remnants of his life, which leads to a new cycle of growth and development—and destruction.

—Brian Moore, *The Black Robe*. New York: Dutton, 1985.

> Father Jean Laforge is a French Jesuit eager to evangelize the Native Canadians in the seventeenth century. Consumed with zeal, he is unprepared first for the rejection of his faith, and then for its complication at the hands of those who wish to be baptized, but for the wrong reasons.

Integrative Discussion Questions for Part One

1. In *Mariette in Ecstasy*, violence—directed by the self toward the body—seems to be a companion along the road to God. And of course, *The Sparrow* and *The Children of God,* as well as *Children of Men*, are marked by very intense violence. How do you evaluate such connections of the spiritual with the violent?

2. In *The Sparrow* and *The Children of God*, Father Sandoz is faced with the possibility of a God who does not respond to real needs, even when the needs are generated out of obedience. By the end of the first novel, Sandoz has in fact lost his faith. In *Mariette in Ecstasy,* Mariette too looks for a withdrawal of Christ from her life, and suggests that this withdrawal is a testing and issues from Christ's true love for her. If these characters were in conversation about the issue of God's silence, how might they respond to each other?

3. In both *Mariette in Ecstasy* and *The Children of Men*, young women believe they are the instruments of God's will. But in both cases, others are skeptical. Xan goes so far as to call Julian a whore. How do we react to these claims? How would Father Sandoz react to these claims? What does it mean to be an instrument of God?

4. The notion that the forms and formulas of faith are comforting even to those whose faith is weak, nonexistent, or faltering is seen in *Mariette in Ecstasy, The Children of God,* and *The Children of Men*. Theo, for instance, continues to attend evensong. What roles do the forms and formulas of faith play in our lives? How might those roles be more authentic?

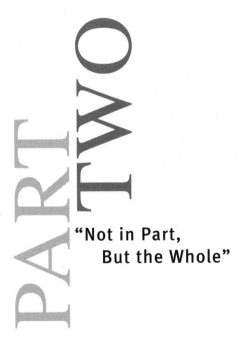

PART TWO

"Not in Part,
But the Whole"

"Not in Part,
But the Whole"

In his essay, "Valmiki's Palm," David James Duncan writes of the fin of a trout which suddenly rises out of his own hand. He is astounded, since he is working in a plastics factory, far from the wild he once loved. But now the wild has arisen in him! In fact, the chemicals of the plant have so charged him that he fails to see that the fin is the edge of a razor blade slicing through his hand. "I grew," he writes, "less vaguely aware"—suggesting that we can live our lives only "vaguely aware," not fully understanding the meaning of what lies directly around us.

Plot lines in novels are often hinged on this limitation: the characters are not omniscient. The narrator may be omniscient, overseeing all—though such narrators have tended to fall away from contemporary fiction. But more often characters move with only partial views, looking for places to set their feet down, but unsure of where the ground may lie. This terrible state of being vaguely aware may propel the plot forward, or may define a character's nature, or may establish the tones of the novel.

And it is uncertainty with which the characters of this section struggle. In Max Allan Collins's graphic novel, *Road to Perdition*, a young boy must reimagine his father, who is so loving at home—and so deadly in his work. In David Guterson's *Snow Falling on Cedars*—a mystery novel, a genre which depends on partial sight—injustice crossing racial and generational lines becomes a personal disaster for people who cannot see in whole. And in Nicole Mazzarella's *This Heavy Silence*, decisions are made with devastating consequences—because the decisions are short-sighted, and seen as if in a glass, darkly. Which is, as St. Paul wrote, how we all see.

PART TWO

SNOW FALLING ON CEDARS David Guterson
(1995)

When Carl Heine is found dead in his gill netting in a bay off the shores of San Pedro Island, suspicion quickly centers on Kabuo Miyamoto, a boyhood friend. Carl's mother had cheated Kabuo out of seven acres of land he and his family had cleared, planted, and cherished. The evidence seems to confirm the suspicion, and Kabuo soon finds himself on trial for his life. But the trial is not just about Kabuo's innocence or guilt. As a thick and terrible snowstorm batters the island, its inhabitants learn that the trial is about the island's past as well.

The island is haunted by its memory of the deportation of its Japanese community to the internment camps set up in the deserts during World War II. That guilt, and the prejudices that grew during the war against the Japanese, are only thinly covered. In addition, those who left to fight either in the European or Pacific theaters struggle with the knowledge of human darkness that they gained during the war. And beyond this, there linger the effects of a strong though forbidden adolescent love between Kabuo's wife, Hatsue, and Ishmael Chambers, who has been driven into emptiness by Hatsue's rejection of him, the horror of the war, and the loss of his arm. As the editor of the island newspaper, he is a journalist who lives by words, but who has no words to speak.

As the trial continues, and as the town struggles to learn what happened out on the waters north of Puget Sound, and as the purifying snowstorm hurls itself against the island— these haunting memories clash against each other. So when

Synopsis

Ishmael Chambers finally learns the truth of that night, he must face not just objective evidence but also the hauntings of his own emptied heart. The trial comes to its abrupt conclusion only when he does so, as the novel ends with the hope that Ishmael's emptiness may somehow be filled.

On the Author

David Guterson (b. 1956) grew up in Seattle, the son of a criminal defense lawyer whose cases provided Guterson with powerful examples of stories. He attended the University of Washington in Seattle, where he decided that he would become a writer. He studied with Charles Johnson and through his tutelage developed his own strong belief that the role of the writer is to present moral questions for reflection. After completing his degrees, Guterson moved to Bainbridge Island in Puget Sound, where he began to teach English at the local high school. Here he discovered Harper Lee's *To Kill a Mockingbird*, which was a formative influence on his writing. He married a year after college and had four children, all of whom he and his wife homeschooled—an account of which appears in his *Family Matters: Why Homeschooling Makes Sense* (1992).

He published his first fiction in 1989: *The Country Ahead of Us, the Country Behind*, and five years later, after ten years of research and crafting, published *Snow Falling on Cedars* (1994), which was a tremendously popular success. It won the PEN/Faulkner Award and was made into a film in 1999. Since then Guterson has published *East of the Mountains* (1999), about a dying man's desire to decide for himself how his life will end, and *Our Lady of the Forest* (2003), about a fictional Marian appearance witnessed by a teenaged girl in Washington. Most of his work is set in

Washington and is deeply informed by that region's vast and rugged beauty.

■ Considering the Novel

David Guterson opens *Snow Falling on Cedars* with a distinctly Christian poem: the opening to *The Inferno* from Dante's *Divine Comedy*. Here the poet, in the middle of his life's journey, finds himself in a dark wood where the straight path is hidden and lost. It is a wild and rough and tangled wood, and even thinking about his predicament again renews the fear that the poet felt when he realized how terribly lost he was. It is a moment of stasis: the poet is still, not moving forward into the plot that awaits him; he has paused, and looks around, fearfully. In terms of meaning, Dante directs the reader's eye to two elements: the wild setting and the state of mind of the character on the journey—which might also be described as wild.

This quotation is apt for *Snow Falling on Cedars*. Here, too, readers will encounter a setting which is vivid and powerful; in fact, the wildness of San Pedro Island will be very present throughout the book. Here, too, readers will also encounter characters in the middle of their life's journey, who become lost in a tangled wood, struggling in stasis, searching for a way to bring meaning back into lives that seem dark and empty.

The novel places the reader in the midst of a trial as convoluted and tangled as Dante's wood: "The accused man, Kabuo Miyamoto, sat proudly upright with a rigid grace, his palms placed softly on the defendant's table—the posture of a man who has detached himself insofar as this is possible at his own trial" (3). The reader soon finds that this is no linear narrative, but a driven plot with amazing and surprising twists and turns that propel the reader on to an equally amazing and surprising revelation and stunning conclusion—though those elements are in the background. The reader finds himself wandering in a tangled wood, moving back and forth in time, reaching to the childhood of some of the characters, reaching, in fact, back to the stories of their parents. If the novel is meant to drive forward at a quick pace, the reader must inevitably be frustrated, for the sensibility is much more composed, much more patient, much more roundabout in its movement toward truth. Does it, in this way, reflect the culture and literary heritage of its Japanese characters?

For a murder mystery, *Snow Falling on Cedars* does something rather remarkable: one hundred and fifty pages before the conclusion, the reader knows how the murdered man died. Once Ishmael Chambers discovers the log notes that show that Carl Heine was thrown from his boat by the bow wave from a large ship coming through the fog, there is no more mystery to be unraveled. Once the characters finally discover the truth and the mystery is solved, the novel which has been so leisurely paced discards its roundabout structure and ends with a startling abruptness: Kabuo is released, they all go home, and Ishmael Chambers sits down to write up an account for his newspaper—all in a very few pages.

Unlike so many mysteries, all is not revealed. Does Kabuo get back the strawberry fields for which he has so yearned, a yearning that pushes much of the narrative? Do Hatsue and Ishmael Chambers have a new relationship? Does Ishmael live again, as Hatsue hopes? What will happen to the family of Carl Heine? None of these questions are definitively answered. By the end of the novel, the woods are still dark—if a little less tangled. The novel seems to ask whether one can ever hope for total light, total clarity, a total untangling. The answer is, No.

But Ishmael Chambers, who is the man of words in this novel, still tries. When the trial concludes and his own work has freed the husband of the woman he loves—or once loved—he sits down to craft a piece that will make sense of what he has seen and heard. He concludes that, first, "[t]he heart of *any* other, because it had a will, would remain forever mysterious" (460); and second, "accident ruled every corner of the universe except the chambers of the human heart" (460). Put together, the insights suggest that the human heart has its conscious purposes, its will, known to each of us—but it is not predictable and is ultimately unknowable to those outside of us. While accident and chance may rule everything else, they cannot govern our own innermost self.

At least, this is what Ishmael Chambers has come to believe. But is it true? Does the novel support his insight? Does, for example, accident rule every corner of the universe? Certainly it seems that accidents are important in the story, but Guterson never leaves the reader with a sense that mere accident or coincidence alone is at play. One of the largest "accidents" of the novel is the snowstorm that sweeps across the island for the duration of the trial. "[T]hose who had lived on the island a long time knew that the storm's outcome was beyond their control. . . . Who knew? Who could predict? If disaster, so be it, they said to themselves. There was nothing to be done except what could be done" (255). So everyone on San Pedro Island is powerfully affected by this accident, and yet the effects depend in large part on the individuals—because there are things that "could be done." Guterson specifically describes those who have prepared by triply securing their boats, or by rationing the kerosene, or by laying in stores, or by simply driving with care and skill. Similarly, the Miyamotos's loss of the strawberry fields may seem to be caused by the "accident" of the war and the subsequent internment of the Japanese community, but at the same time, the loss of those fields comes about because of a deliberate choice by Etta Heine. The most prominent "accident" seems to be the bow wave that drops Carl Heine from his spar on a foggy night, but Guterson questions the accidental nature of even that event, since Carl Heine climbs to the mast because of his desire to save the lantern: "And so he paid for his fastidious nature, his compulsion to keep things perfect. He paid because he had inherited from his mother a certain tightness through the purse strings" (457). Guterson suggests that there is no such thing as pure accident; no action results only from outside forces.

But is there then pure human will? At first it seems that there may be. Again, the trial, the narrator suggests, "unlike the storm was a human affair, stood squarely in the arena of human responsibility, was no mere accident of wind and sea but instead a thing humans could make sense of. Its progress, its impact, its outcome, its meaning—these were in the hands of people" (313). But even here, accident is involved. All of the evidence suggests Kabuo's guilt, but the storm itself provides the reason for the truth coming out. The storm leads Ishmael Chambers to seek out weather records, which leads him to seek out records for the night of Carl Heine's death, which leads him to the truth of Carl's death. The truth did not come out before, simply because the two men who had logged in the information had been randomly transferred the next day. Even apparently human events are shrouded in mystery.

But the novel asks a more powerful question, one which Ishmael Chambers does not explicitly answer: if accident does not govern the chambers of the human heart, then what does?

Multiple suggestions and answers are affirmed by Guterson. Ishmael Chambers's mother argues that faith governs the human heart. "You felt Him as a child" (342) she insists when Ishmael expresses his deep unhappiness; certainly her own sense of God's governing presence is easy and sure: "Everybody knows what God is" (342), she insists. But her clarity is not shared by Ishmael;

his own feelings as a child were those of a child; he no longer senses God—and he cannot generate a sense of God if nothing prompts him: "I can't make a feeling like that up, can I? Maybe God just chooses certain people, and the rest of us—we can't feel Him" (342). When his mother affirms that she has prayed for him, he reminds her that boys prayed in the war, too. "They still got killed, Mother. Just like the guys who didn't pray. It didn't matter either way" (347).

The heart may also be governed by the dictates of one's community. When Hatsue and Ishmael are young and meeting inside the cedar tree, they believe themselves to be in love. But Hatsue is uneasy. She knows that she is disobeying her parents, who demand that she see herself first as Japanese, and who, she knows, would never accept her claim of love for a non-Japanese boy. It would seem, at this point, that the narrative is about to follow a Romeo and Juliet plotline. But Hatsue herself recognizes the wrongness of their relationship because it is outside the boundaries of her cultural tradition; she calls what they are doing "evil" (175). Ishmael distances the evil from them: he insists that the world is evil, in its prejudice and racial bias (175). But when they begin to make love inside the tree, Hatsue knows that something essential is not right—and she pulls away. Conversely, when she makes love on her wedding night with Kabuo, she knows that something is very, very right. She tries, unsuccessfully, to communicate this to Ishmael, and though her final image of him is that of "a handsome boy with one arm outstretched, beckoning her to come back" (215), her deep sense of her place within a community makes her leave him and take up a role she instinctively knows to be the right one. Her mother, in the internment camp, insists that her experience should teach her "something about the darkness in the hearts of the *hakujin*" (200), and though Hatsue resists this understanding, she does affirm her mother's sense that there is an essential distinction between the two worlds that cannot be bridged.

The heart may be governed by a sense of justice. Ishamel Chambers's father stands as a positive model—and ultimately, it will be this model that will lead Ishmael to make the decision to turn over the notes he has discovered that, in them, will free Kabuo. His father, who founded the newspaper that Ishamel now publishes, writes powerful editorials against the Japanese internments—editorials that lead to physical threats against him. But his sense of justice overwhelms those threats, even though the editorials, in the end, do not stop the deportations. His strong use of words to motivate and activate, distinguishes him—and creates a model that Ishmael Chambers admires enormously, but cannot live up to. The negative example of a heart unmoved by a sense of justice is Etta Heine, sharp and miserly, considered "hateful" by the community, whose prejudice against the Japanese is unreasoning and deep. She knows that the Miyamoto family is only one payment away from acquiring the land, yet when they are deported and unable to make the final payment, and when her husband dies and the decision falls to her, she sends their money back and sells the land at an even larger profit to another islander—who is not Japanese. She has, Kabuo points out to her, done nothing illegal, but she has nonetheless done something wrong. In her prejudice, she will not admit this, and so comes to blame Kabuo for her son's death.

There are other answers that Guterson suggests. The heart may be ruled by a quest for truth, as suggested by the character of Art Moran, who follows the evidence when it leads to Kabuo and who willingly follows it when it clears the suspect; and Nels Gudmundsson, the attorney who, in the midst of his own shrinking life, fights for the freedom of Kabuo. The heart may be ruled by passion, as is the case with Ishmael Chambers and Susan Marie Heine. The heart may be ruled by fear, as is the case with the nation, as it interns a portion of its own populace. The heart may be ruled by prejudice, as Kabuo's reserve and dignity in the courtroom are seen as manifestations not of an inner calm and tranquility but of the remorseless severity of the Japanese soldier—an enemy. There seem to be so many potential answers for what governs the heart, that the final choice itself seems one that is merely accidental.

But there is one refrain that Guterson plays again and again, one strong suggestion for what governs the human heart, and which Ishmael Chambers (Is his last name a play on this question?) himself might at least unconsciously affirm: the human heart is ruled, ultimately, by the desire for the good life. It is the good life that the characters so desperately seek, and it is the good life which seems to recede from them—or which has been taken from them. This desire centers most fully on the three men intimately connected through the trial—Carl Heine, Kabuo Miyamoto, and Ishmael Chambers—who all share the experience of the war—an experience that affects them quite similarly. Each of them is confronted by darkness and emptiness and silence, and for Kabuo and Ishmael, the trial brings to a point the spiritual crisis which has governed them for ten years.

Guterson stresses this crisis through repetition. Noting that after the war, Carl Heine was no longer the jocular boy he had been, but was silent and still. Guterson writes, "What could he say to others? There was no longer any speaking for the hell of it, no opening one's mouth just to have it open, and if others would read darkness into his silence, well then, darkness was there, wasn't it?" (54). Carl tells his wife that "since the war he couldn't *speak*" (297). And because of this, he is a lonely man, even in the midst of his family.

Kabuo cannot recover from his killing of a German boy, a solider, who dies slowly and painfully and pitifully beside him. Everything else fades into unreality, a "nuisance" (154) he endures as he focuses on that dying boy. "His face had been molded by his experiences as a soldier, and he appeared to the world seized up inside precisely because this was how he felt" (154). Hatsue recognizes this spiritual grief. She understands that "the war had elicited in him a persistent guilt that lay on his soul like a shadow" (359).

Ishmael Chambers, too, has confronted darkness. During the snowstorm, he drives past the seven acres that Kabuo is so eager to own—his own hope to return to the peace and fullness of his childhood—and he sees that the world has obliterated all boundary distinctions. "The world was one world, and the notion that a man might kill another over some small patch of it did not make sense" (321). Then the narrator pauses and considers, because suddenly for Ishamel it does make sense: "Ishmael knew that such things happened. He had been to war, after all" (321). For Ishmael, the horror of the war is connected with his loss of Hatsue, and together, they have left him empty. He waits now for something, some sort of return. But he cannot define what this might look like (325).

In such a haunted and broken world, in a world that is dark and cold and empty and silent, what rules the chambers of the heart? The desire for the good life, the yearning for the good life, wherever it might be found. In *Snow Falling on Cedars*, the good life is found primarily in the family—in the solace, grace, generosity, communion, intimacies, and love of the family. Guterson stresses those moments when Carl is surrounded by his home. It is a blunt, no-nonsense home, but the inside is lovely, welcoming, with large furniture, burnished walls, rafters open in the ceiling, and filled with Susan Marie's hospitality. There are children, and Guterson points to the work they do with their father—culling raspberry canes. He points to them sitting together in church. He points to the close sexual intimacies between Carl and Susan Marie, and the grace and thoughtfulness that the large and strong Carl Heine brings to his lovemaking. He is defined on the island as "the *good* man," by which they mean "the silent-toiling, autonomous gill-netter" (38), the respected fisherman who worked alone; "other men admired him because he was powerful and good at his work, because on the sea he was thoroughly competent and even in his rough way elegantly so" (53). But it is within the context of his family that he is most fully himself, and the images of him on the boat—which, in fact, do not show great competence—are paired with the image of him carrying his hurt six-year-old son to the doctor, holding him while the stitches go in, and then carrying him away "in the cradling manner one holds an infant" (53).

Kabuo, too, finds the governing of his heart in his family. Sitting in his cell, separated from his wife and children, he reflects on their meaning for him. "He saw only darkness after the war, in the world and in his own soul, everywhere but in the smell of strawberries, in the good scent of his wife and of his three children, a boy and two girls, three gifts. He felt he did not deserve for a moment the happiness his family brought to him" (169). Like Carl, he desires to return to the land and the smell of the strawberries of his light-filled past. And though he is frustrated in this—and there is no guarantee at the end of the novel that this will be achieved—he is also supported by a loving wife, who "brought herself to his sorrow completely, not to console him but to give him time to become himself again" (359). There is no real consolation she can offer, but she can offer herself and help to take on his burden. "She sat across from him at the kitchen table at three o'clock in the morning, while he stared in silence or talked or wept, and she took, when she could, a piece of his sorrow and stored it for him in her own heart" (360); she is, for him, an agent of grace, his one light in darkness. When she brings the news of her pregnancy to him, Kabuo's only response had been a renewal of his determination to get his farm back (362). But prison and the trial and his near-death have changed his perspective. He recognizes the power of his gifts. Thus at the novel's end, Kabuo has changed; he does not return home ready and determined to resume the fight for the seven acres of strawberry fields; instead, he walks out of the prison without shackles and "he kissed his wife for a long time" (454)—the last we see of him.

Ishmael Chambers, however, has none of this. He has only the memory of his lost love for Hatsue, a memory constantly grinding against the moments when he now sees her around the island, holding Kabuo's children. "[S]ometimes I wonder if unfairness isn't . . . part of things, I wonder if we should even expect fairness, if we should assume we have some sort of right to it" (325), he complains to Hatsue during the trial. And though Ishmael is using these words to attack what he sees as her rejecting him, he is also uttering his own sense of the world: There seems to be little justice at all in it. It does seem all mere accident. And in such a world, is it such an unpardonable thing to reach out to someone he loves, even if he does it by withholding evidence that will clear her husband? It was only an accident, after all, that he came across the log account. Thus rationalization tries to fill and cover emptiness—but it cannot.

When Ishmael begs his mother to tell him what to do in his unhappiness, her answer is the one that Carl Heine and Kabuo Miyamoto have found, though she couches the answer in her own frustration: "I've tried to understand what it's been like for you—having gone to war, having lost your arm, not having married or had children. I've tried to make sense of it all, believe me, I have—how it must feel to be you" (347). But, she notes, while others returned and married and raised families "despite whatever was behind them," Ishmael went "numb" (347). "When it comes down to it," she tells her son, "here's what you should do about being unhappy: you should get married and have some children" (348). Ishmael dismisses this as simplistic, but his mother will not accept his easy rejection. In fact, neither will Hatsue, who, after Ishmael comes to bring her the new evidence of the bow wave, gives him exactly the same advice: "Find someone to marry. . . . Have children, Ishmael. Live" (446).

Here is the good life in *Snow Falling on Cedars*. It lies in the images of Carl Heine clasping Susan Marie to him in their burnished living room, and in the bare-chested children playing among the raspberries outside. It lies in the home of Kabuo and Hatsue, in their child taking her first steps for her imprisoned father, in the long kiss that comes between the freed man and his grace-filled wife. It is the drive for this good life—and the recognition that the good life can come in the present, and need not always be tied to the past—that rules the chambers of the human heart.

This is not an easy solution to the question for Guterson. In fact, the complicated world of the novel seems on some level to be entirely random, and the directions of the heart subject to forces that it cannot govern. In his summation, Nels Gudmundsson notes that fate has acted against Kabuo. "There are things in this universe that we cannot control" (418), he admits. And certainly, human frailty has its play. "We hate one another; we are the victims of irrational fears. And there is nothing in the stream of human history to suggest we are going to change this" (418–19). Ishmael Chambers agrees and adds to this sense the knowledge of a God "who stood at the wayside indifferently while Eric Bledsoe bled to death in the surf, and then there was that boy on the deck of the hospital ship with the blood soaking his groin"

(425). History, he judges, "was whimsical and immune to private yearnings" (425).

Against these claims of randomness and frailty and hatred are the words of Ishmael's father, who warned his son about hatred on an island; living constricted made people vulnerable to hate, but also emphasized the importance of walking with care, given that the sea bounds them all and keeps them close together. He "trusted God to guide their hearts, though he knew them to be vulnerable to hate" (439). At the end of the novel, the word *heart* is used repeatedly to suggest something weak and yet strong, subject to hatred and frailty, yet open to grace and powerful goodness. Hatsue's father had spoken of Ishmael in this way to his own father: "We believe his heart is strong, like his father's. Your son is a very good boy" (441). In writing her letter of farewell, Hatsue tells Ishmael that "[y]our heart is large and you are gentle and kind, and I know you will do great things in this world" (442). And Ishmael comes to recognize that his frequent visits to his mother, which he believes were meant to support her, "were as much for his own heart as they were for hers; he had fooled himself for years into thinking otherwise" (443). All of these references come quickly, one upon another, and lead to Ishmael's rejection of hatred and frailty, to his governance of the chambers of his own heart, and to his decision to bring the record log to Hatsue's family.

There are things we cannot control, suggests Guterson. There are irrational fears, and we can be haunted. There is frailty. And there is hatred. But perhaps, the novel suggests, it is these that are the real accidents. Perhaps in the end, with grace and love and the solace of others, they need not rule the chambers of the human heart.

▓ Discussion Questions about the Novel

1. How does the setting of San Pedro Island itself affect the plot action of the novel? How does it contribute to shaping the characters? Guterson claims that the ocean confines, and the water that laps around the land reveals little (39). Are we to take this as evocative of the characters, too? Or is this meant to evoke something about the mystery that is being unraveled?

2. One way to read this novel is as a thick anthropological description of a specific small island whose isolation binds several cultural groups closely together—first- and second-generation Japanese Americans, Caucasian settlers who make their homes on the island, and the summer people who boat up from Seattle. Is it helpful to read the novel in this way, or as a work of historical fiction detailing a shameful moment in American history? Which reading does a better job of shedding light on the meaning of the novel's concluding line?

3. We don't know what happens to the seven acres of strawberry fields. Will Ishmael Chambers be prosecuted for withholding evidence? Will there be healing between the three principal families of the novel? Why does Guterson leave so much to the reader to fill in?

4. We are told that things in the community of San Pedro are not shaped by talk; the image that is held in most esteem is that of the silent fisherman, alone at night, working by himself. So if things are not shaped by talk, what are they shaped by?

5. Japanese poetry, which the title evokes, depends for its meaning on the impressions it creates. It works by connecting the human world with the natural world, so that human truth

comes through observing the details of the natural world. In Guterson's novel, the natural world is evoked in the delicate snow falling from the sky, the thrashing snow, the covered cedar branches, the old rich cedars growing from the earth. What meaning does this set of impressions convey to you?

6. *Snow Falling on Cedars* is a murder mystery, also a love story, and a courtroom drama. Each of these genres is conventional, with strong expectations of how they should proceed. Does Guterson follow these conventions, or undercut them, or use them in some other way to craft his novel?

7. One way to describe the movement of this novel is linear: the trial proceeds, the evidence is given, the trial is resolved. Another way to understand that movement is circular, where the past keeps intersecting with and impacting the present. How do these two ways of moving—and of living—mix in the novel? Does the lack of linear progress frustrate the reader?

▓ Other Books to Consider

—Tony Earley, *Jim the Boy*. Boston: Little, Brown, 2000.

> Young Jim, whose father has died and who is now being raised by his mother and three uncles, begins to come of age in the early 1930s. Still young, he senses nonetheless the powerful pull of his own past and his strong connections to the land.

—Joy Kogawa, *Obasan*. Toronto: Lester & Dennys, 1981.

> *Obasan* is a fictionalized memoir that recounts the author's family's relocation from the western coast of Canada to a camp in Alberta, where her father was forced to labor on sugar beet farms to serve the war effort.

—Jerome Lawrence and Robert E. Lee, *Inherit the Wind*. New York: Random House, 1951, 1955.

In this dramatization of the famous Scopes trial, Lawrence and Lee explore the ways that a courtroom drama can uncover not only evidence, but also the chambers of the human heart and its motivations.

—Bernard Malamud, *The Natural*. New York: Farrar, Straus, 1952.

Perhaps one of the greatest baseball novels ever written, *The Natural* follows the story of Roy Hobbes, whose natural talent promises to make him one of the greatest players in the game. But a wrong turn during his giddy upward movement blunts his greatness, and when he finally finds his way back to the game he loves, he is dogged by his past.

—Annie Proulx, *The Shipping News*. New York: Scribner, 1993.

Released from the psychological and emotional abuse of his family and his wife through their deaths, Quoyle, the unlikely protagonist of this lyrical novel, moves with his two daughters and aunt to Killick-Claw on the coast of Newfoundland, where he begins to write for the local newspaper. Having been defeated in all he has done, it seems unlikely that he will prosper here. But as he frees himself from the ghosts of his past, he begins to grow into full humanity, astonishing no one more than himself.

THIS HEAVY SILENCE
Nicole Mazzarella

(2005)

Synopsis

One winter night in 1962, thirty-eight-year-old Dottie
Connell answers the doorbell to find her best friend, Zela
Brubaker Morgan, on the porch with her young daughter,
Mattie, in tow. When Zela later kills her abusive husband
and commits suicide, Dottie finds herself the reluctant
guardian of a small child. A farmer by trade, Dottie has been
working single-mindedly to pay off the mortgage on the 300-
acre family farm, which is held by her greedy Uncle Charlie.
Despite, or perhaps because of, her father's resistance
to passing the inheritance down to a daughter, Dottie is
determined to protect and redeem her land.

Eight-year-old Mattie is not only a distraction to the
rhythm of hard work the farm demands, but she also brings
emotional complications in the shape of her Uncle Morris,
Dottie's former fiancé, and Morris's elegant, red-headed wife
Charlotte. Although Dottie seems to lack motherly instincts
and struggles simply to care for Mattie's basic needs, her
hired hand, Stanley, parents the child with gentleness and
good humor. He also works hard to open up Dottie's own
battered and wary heart. The novel is divided into two parts.
The first ends after Dottie is able to purchase her farm from
Uncle Charlie with funds that belong to Mattie, the second
begins ten years later and traces the consequences of that
decision. As the novel concludes, Dottie is forced to consider
her life, the choices she has made, and the means by which
she might make amends to those she has injured.

Nicole Mazzarella (b. 1975), a Midwestern writer who now lives in Illinois, grew up in Ohio. She received a MFA in creative writing from Old Dominion University in Virginia and has taught creative writing at the college level. *This Heavy Silence,* her first novel, is influenced by her own family history. Her great-grandmother, also a writer, gave her pen name to the farm where her grandmother was raised and where her great-aunt and great-uncle still live—Maplewood Farm in the Pleasant Valley of Lucas, Ohio. The character of Dottie originally appeared in two short stories, as a young child attending her brother's funeral and as a woman jilted by her fiancé. Mazzarella has said that when she decided to develop Dottie's character, the first draft of the novel followed her from birth to death at age seventy; in the final version, the author focused on two key years in Dottie's life. *This Heavy Silence* won the Paraclete Press Fiction Award in 2004, a Christy Award, and a fiction award from *Christianity Today.*

Considering the Novel

On a Sunday morning shortly after Mattie Morgan comes to live with Dottie Connell, the two engage in a titanic battle of wills. It isn't the first such battle, nor is it to be the last, but it does reveal in a single scene the nearly unbridgeable chasm that lies between them. Just as Dottie has relaxed into her reading chair and opened her farm account books, Mattie comes dancing down the stairs, wearing a new lavender dress with deep purple ties. Her hair is freshly shampooed, she has clamped blue butterfly barrettes beside her long bangs, and now she pulls white gloves primly across her small hands. "I heard church bells," she announces to Dottie. "Church always starts at ten-thirty. We're going to be late." The rest of the conversation is short but predictable.

"We're not going."

"Why not?"

Silence.

"It's Sunday."

"Which isn't any different from Monday or Tuesday. You might as well change your clothes" (65–68).

Which Mattie eventually does, but only after having stared Dottie down for nearly an hour. The contrasts between the town-bred child and the middle-aged farmer could hardly be more striking. Mattie adores soft, pretty things, delicate smells, beautiful colors and shapes. She enjoys her friends, and church is one place where she can see them. She expects the tidy, orderly rhythm of her life to cough up unanticipated pleasures—like a new lavender dress. Dottie, on the other hand, has bound herself to a single rule by which she measures everything: Is it practical? Will it help her save the farm? The lavender dress with its rows of lace is clearly impractical, as is the notion of taking a day off from work. Sunday is a day to settle accounts, to record credits and debits, to plot a new year with higher profits. It is useless to waste it on "friends," who will only gossip and betray, let alone on the God who snatches away brothers, lovers, and fathers and whose capricious weather plays havoc with every farmer's careful plans. It is useless to explain all this to Mattie; better just to be silent.

Yet despite their contrasting personalities and desires, Mattie and Dottie are linked by inseparable bonds. Chief among these is their shared history: not only is Mattie the child of Dottie's best friend, she is the niece of Dottie's lover, the child she and Morris might have had together. As Mattie confronts Dottie with her demand to attend church, Dottie thinks, "[S]he argued like her Uncle Morris, casually, without the thought of losing" (68). But Mattie is also like Dottie herself. Even though she looks and smells like Charlotte, with her new dress and lilac-scented hair, it is Dottie's stubborn determination that most characterizes Mattie. She matches silence with silence, scrutinizing Dottie "with her arms crossed . . . until the cuckoo whistled the quarter hour and then the half hour" (68) before admitting defeat at 11:00. And Mattie and Dottie are linked, too, by the fact that Zela deliberately left the guardianship of her small daughter to Dottie, and a little girl cannot simply be abandoned, no matter how difficult or inconvenient she may be. It is Mattie's vulnerability, undeniable even to Dottie as she notices the child's uncombed hair, that forces Dottie to take on responsibilities other than her farm: the tangles, she thinks, suggest that Mattie "did not have a mirror or a mother" (66). So Dottie assumes the debt of caring for Mattie, as she had assumed the debt her father left on the farm and as he, before her, had assumed the debt his own father had bequeathed to him.

Debts alone do not make a relationship, however, and two people so very stubborn and so very much alike need a mediator. They find him in Stanley, the hired man. Although Dottie and Mattie are both born to the land—Mattie is a member of the powerful Brubaker clan and Dottie is farming her great-grandfather's 300 acres—it is Stanley, the outsider, who settles most comfortably into the landscape. And it is Stanley who provides the emotional ballast for both females. We first encounter him the morning of Mattie's parents' funeral, when Dottie hauls the child out to the machine shed, determined to combat grief with the only antidote she knows—hard work. Dottie gives Mattie the task of throwing trash into the incinerator, which she reluctantly does, one envelope at a time. But when Stanley comes in, he picks up an entire box and dumps it into the fire. "Little one, you go play," he says (35), setting the tone for all his encounters with Mattie. He is the one who feeds her caramel candies, and coaxes her to milk the cow, and eats supper with her in his little house, and admires her new dresses. Later he will drive her to school and play Scrabble with her on Wednesday nights. Indeed, he slides into such a natural relationship with Mattie that Dottie imagines he must have fathered children of his own, since he so obviously possesses the parental instinct she lacks. She envies his easy camaraderie and that of "mothers who had nine months to grow accustomed to the weight of a child and whose hollowed wombs created an instinct to remember their children" (49).

Stanley's relationship with Dottie is more complicated. He respects her as his boss and keeps his hands to himself, unlike some of her previous hired help, but even before he finally tells her that he loves her (ten years after he has come to work for her), we sense their mutual attraction. When they are in the machine shed with Mattie, Dottie notices "the flecks of ash" in his hair, smells his warm breath, and worries that she isn't feeding him enough. Later when they are milking cows, Stanley shakes the snow off his head onto a giggling Mattie and then turns to shower Dottie with flakes in a scene that can only be called flirtatious. Perhaps because Stanley sees Dottie as desirable, we too are able to look beyond the brusque, abrupt woman she has become to the passionate person she once was. The glimpses of her earlier life that we catch throughout the novel become, then, more credible and more poignant: the ten-year-old giggling over ice cream with Zela at Palmer's Drug Store; the adoring little sister watching her brother fall to his death from the high beam of the barn; the lover watching her fiancé march away to war; the young woman shocked to see him step off the train four years later with a new red-headed fiancée in tow; the daughter struggling to earn her father's respect; the farmer obsessed with owning her family's land. But these glimpses of a warm and vibrant woman—a woman who "had her time in the hay"—are just that: glimpses. And we as readers may find ourselves hard pressed to love her as well as Stanley does.

Dottie is not, however, without tender moments. When she learns that Mattie has been talking to Charlotte on the outside phone, complaining about her hard life on the farm, Dottie decides to discipline her with some stern words and a wooden spoon. It isn't just that Mattie has confided in Charlotte, the "other" woman in Morris's life, but that Mattie has exposed Dottie's failings to everyone on the party line, and through them to the entire community. But when Dottie finds Mattie in the bathroom, bunching her hair into clumps as she tries to recreate the braids her mother always plaited, she lays down the spoon and picks up a comb. Confronted by such fierce helplessness, Dottie's memory—and instinct—take over. As she braids Mattie's hair, she tells her stories about her mother, about the French braid Zela wore for her first date and the fishbone braid she, in turn, plaited down Dottie's back. For once the heavy silence is broken. "I took my time," Dottie recalls, "smoothing each strand, checking the sides to keep them even, but still I finished too quickly" (75).

Such moments of intimacy are rare. For too long—over seventeen years—Dottie's love has been funneled into her farm; her attention, since her father's death, has been focused on putting money into the envelope that lies on top of the refrigerator, the envelope labeled "My Land." But the farm will only become "My Land" if she keeps working, if she never allows the monotonous beat—work work work work—to slow down, if she never allows herself to become distracted. Work has become her drug, her addiction, her explanation, her cure for every pain. She keeps three cows not because they contribute substantially to her annual income but simply because she "hated empty barns and slow winters" (6). She organizes her kitchen like her machine shed, the most useful pans hung from nails above the stove where she can quickly reach them and put them to work.

Work is necessary, of course: land left untilled quickly reverts to the wild; cows left unmilked die, but work can also keep life—and God—at bay. It is the hedge against both regrets and loneliness: "Work," she thinks, "only soothed by moving too fast to think" (33). But such ruthless efficiency scrubs away ordinary human connections. There is no space in Dottie's kitchen for the give and take of the "funeral brigade," the women who gather together to feed the grieving and chew over the most recent gossip. "I had worked too hard to suddenly need them," she says, justifying her lack of hospitality when they crowd into her kitchen to prepare meals for the orphaned Mattie (53). When the roots of an old spruce tree crack her drainpipe and muddy water leaks into her basement, she fires up the backhoe, digs a trench, and starts hauling out stones, pushing herself to the brink of exhaustion without once summoning her hired hand. "Of course, you do not ask for help," Stanley says when he discovers her working past dark, and even Dottie doesn't know if he speaks "with irritation or admiration" (169). And Morris, trying to account for the failure of their love affair, can only say to her, "The truth is I never loved farming. When I met Charlotte, I saw new possibilities" (237).

Little wonder, then, that Dottie sees Mattie as a major distraction from the work at hand. "I would never have taken on a child who will only slow me down," Dottie tells Morris on his first trip to the farm (43). And Mattie brings not just her eight-year-old self, but a whole host of other complications into Dottie's life: reminders of her love affair with Morris; confrontations with Charlotte, whom she has successfully avoided for many years; and most alarmingly the reappearance of her cousin Rex, summoned home by his father, Uncle Charlie, to take over the Connell family farm. Faced with foreclosure, Dottie begins a series of desperate moves to keep both Mattie and the farm, even going as far as to attend the Presbyterian church one Sunday morning where she tries belatedly to learn the art of mothering. She awkwardly helps Mattie with her coat, although she is "old enough to do it on her own," but later finds herself perplexed when the preacher commends Jesus for sleeping during the storm on the Sea of Galilee and calls the disciples "faithless," since it is obvious to Dottie that if the disciples "had simply waited for God to save them, their ship would have sunk in the storm" (112, 114). Dottie has no intention of waiting for God to help her.

Yet it is in church that Dottie first admits she might be willing to borrow against the money Zela left for Mattie. It is in church that Dottie confronts Rex and discovers his asking price for the farm: $300,000, a sum so high that even Dottie gasps, "It's not worth that" (116). Except that it is—to Dottie and to Uncle Charlie, who already knows the exact amount of Mattie's inheritance, and to Rex who will not settle for less. Dottie, like the disciples, does not wait for God to wake up and save her, but takes matters into her on hands. She arranges to meet Rex at the courthouse, she takes $500 from her seed money to bribe the lawyer Zela had employed to write her will, and she prepares to mortgage Mattie's future for the farm. Instinct takes over. She barely hesitates before withdrawing the entire amount of Mattie's inheritance, writing Rex's name on a cashier's check, and taking possession of the title to the farm.

But if Dottie doesn't hesitate, do we? What are we to make of her decision to spend $300,000 on a farm that is not worth half that amount? Before she is threatened with immediate foreclosure and before she knows the amount of Mattie's inheritance, Dottie rigorously refutes any notion that she might use the child's money to finance her own obsession. When Morris says, "[D]on't act like you wouldn't use the inheritance to get this farm in your name," she throws him out of the house (43). But when she actually comes face to face with the possibility of losing the land and with the reality of enough money to free her from that threat, she fulfills Morris's prediction to the letter. It is a conscious choice, but perhaps the habit of putting the farm before every other love has also become an instinct. Although Dottie insists to herself that everything she does, she does for Mattie, it is difficult to separate that explanation from the fact that she can now throw away the monthly envelope marked "My Land" and instead simply say, "This is My Land."

It is ironic that Mattie's arrival both precipitates the crisis—it is because Uncle Charlie knows Dottie has access to $300,000 that he has promised that amount to Rex—and relieves it. But Dottie has forgotten that debts can rarely be paid in full. It was a truth she had realized when she looked at the account books and recognized that the mortgage her father had signed over to Uncle Charlie was far more than the farm could ever produce. "He had known," Dottie thinks, "that I would never earn enough to own this land" (98). So in spending Mattie's inheritance for land that isn't worth $300,000, Dottie has simply replaced one debt for another. "Once [Mattie] turns eighteen," the lawyer tells her, "you must give her the remaining money" (121). But there will be no remaining money; indeed, unless there is a miracle, there will probably be no money at all, a fact that Dottie, who has farmed all her life, knows in her very bones. Mattie's inheritance will be the farm, not soulless cash, and Dottie recognizes that she must insure that Mattie will come to love the farm as she herself does.

But Mattie also deserves something more immediate. As Dottie leaves the bank, she looks around at the stores nearby. There is a wig shop and a women's dress shop. Neither is promising. So she enters the camera shop and buys a Brownie 44a with three aperture settings and a single-speed shutter for the extravagant price of $35.00. She wraps it in lavender-flowered paper and leaves it on the kitchen table for Mattie to find—a silent, conciliatory gesture, payment in advance for the debt she has incurred.

Debt figures not only in Dottie's personal life but also in her relationship—or lack therefore—with God. As a child, she felt only the heavy obligation of not living up to God's expectations. God, she surmised, liked "quiet children best and daughters who wore dresses and smiled often. He wanted us to sit up straight and not laugh too loudly" (67). But as Dottie matures, the roles shift. God now stands in Dottie's debt, having failed to meet her expectations. At her brother's funeral she recognizes that "God's faithfulness did not seem great" (106), and she comes to see him as one who takes away whatever she most desperately loves and desires. Yet, even so, she cannot quite muster up "enough faith to stop believing in Him entirely" (67).

Ten years pass, and the second half of the novel begins with a word we have come to expect: "Working." Although it is 1972, not much has changed. Maintaining the farm requires the combined efforts of Dottie, Stanley, and Mattie, all of whom persist in the habits they have already established. Dottie puts in long hours, wresting a living from her blackberry vines and fields, and trying to keep herself and the farm from falling further into debt. Stanley tends the fields and Mattie with equal patience and care. Mattie works when she must, snatching bits of beauty with her camera and moments of pleasure with her boyfriend, Travis. It comes as no surprise to anyone who has been a mother or a daughter that tensions between Dottie and Mattie escalate as Mattie pushes through her adolescence. Nor is it a surprise that the flashpoint should be sex.

Early in the second half of the novel, Dottie and Mattie have an uncomfortable conversation about the "facts of life." They are in Mattie's bedroom, painting their nails—a setting seemingly so unnatural for Dottie that readers, like Mattie herself, may have trouble picturing her there. Later Mattie lashes out, "I will not be a bitter, old virgin like you" (156). But Dottie is not a virgin; indeed Mattie's awakening sexuality brings back memories of her own passionate affair with Morris, of the mud beneath their toes, and the smell of his breath, and the way her flesh "took on the shape of a woman under his hands" (135). Nor does "bitter" seem quite the right word to describe her. Betrayed? Harsh? Wary? Hardheaded, perhaps, a term that Stanley uses? As readers, even though we have access to her own thoughts, perceptions, and memories, we struggle to understand Dottie and her fierce determination to push people away. Dottie also struggles to understand herself, and her reluctance to talk with Mattie about sex. "Prudery did not account for my euphemisms," she thinks, "but lack of conversations did" (129). She settles for a shorthand version of *A Young Lady's Private Counselor*, the book her mother had substituted for a frank conversation about sex, now refracted through the lens of her own habitual understanding of the world: "Nothing good comes from a man finding you pretty," she tells Mattie. And the cure for desire is "hard work," an antidote, she admits to herself, that she has found particularly ineffective (132, 134).

The lens through which Mattie looks, however, is not hard work. Rather, it belongs to her beloved camera, which offers her the freedom to frame the world as she sees it—bits and pieces of beauty caught in a wild turkey's long neck, or a kitten's watery eyes, or the droop of a single petal. It is a world that Dottie, despite her fierce love for her farm and everything on it, cannot see, although each week she looks through the three rolls of developed film she picks up from the Shutter Bug, rifling through the pictures for tell-tale signs of a boyfriend. After ten years of living together, Mattie and Dottie still communicate obliquely— through the pictures they "share," the long walks around the farm that Dottie must bribe Mattie to take, the mutual affection they have for Stanley. Dottie's forty-eighth birthday party reveals just how tenuous all these connections remain. Despite the promise of the evening—Stanley's neatly plastered hair, Dottie's pearl necklace and earrings, Mattie's special dinner—it remains only a promise. Stanley and Dottie go for a drive together, but as they wind through the country roads they inevitably turn back to the farm: where else would Dottie want to be? She cannot see beyond the land and its never-ending demands; Stanley can neither stop loving Dottie nor settle for their unconsummated relationship; Mattie has only been waiting to turn eighteen to claim her inheritance, unaware that it is locked in the land she is desperate to leave behind. There is no easy escape from the lives they have made for themselves or from the silences that have hardened into habit.

As the novel draws to a close, it invites us to think about these silences. There are the silences of love—Dottie's certainty that she need not tell Morris she loves him, will marry him, will fight for him because their bodies have already said all that needs to be said. There are the silences of companionship, of working side by side, that Dottie shares with Stanley and that she thinks she shares with Mattie. Work and duty, we discover, can be the language of love. But the silences of love and companionship communicate richly only when there are no misunderstandings, no breaches, no possibility of misinterpretation—and how often are we assured of that? The silence of failed expectation, the silence of fear, the silence of misplaced patience—it just isn't the right time yet to speak—all these silences deform relationships and raise barriers that are nearly impossible to cross. These are the silences that isolate Dottie from her family and friends and from God, even when she longs to break them. "I never prayed for God's help in what I could do myself," she thinks, "but occasionally my prayers joined with others in the valley for the weather." But then she remembers that "the heaviness of the silence that followed the prayers felt as immense as God . . . [and] the silence settled on me like an accusation" (181–82).

Such silence breeds more silence. Looking at a distant Mattie in the aftermath of an argument, Dottie recalls that "[a]s a child she had used silence instinctively, as if she would perfect the technique with age, and she had" (139). The silence of punishment is never so keenly felt as when Mattie leaves the house in the middle of the night, moves to Mansfield, marries Travis, and becomes a mother—all without a word to Dottie. And when Stanley reaches the end of his patience with Dottie, he says simply, "I know you won't believe me," and sets out for Florida, leaving a vacant silence in his wake.

But it is also Stanley who breaks the silence before he leaves, who dares to speak the truth that Dottie must hear: "Love keeps no record of wrong," he tells her. "Yet you, Dottie, keep records so long they run together, and one man pays another man's debt" (216). Dottie's love for the land—and for Mattie and Stanley and Morris—has been polluted by a keeping of accounts as perverse as that of Uncle Charlie. There is nothing Morris can say to Dottie to justify his abandonment, nothing Stanley can do to convince her of his love, nothing Mattie can do to please her. Their debts are insurmountable, as is the debt she feels God owes to her. Yet her own great debt, incurred when she spends Mattie's inheritance, remains unacknowledged until the night she opens up her account book for 1962, darkens the line between Mattie and Rex's names, writes "*My Record of Wrongs*" and then prays into the silence: "I've made a mess of things. I'm sorry" (231).

To Dottie, it may have "hardly seemed like a prayer," but it is a confession ratified by repentance as she begins to make changes large and small: she sells five-acre parcels of the farm to finance

Mattie and Travis's relocation to California, enjoys a moment of reunion with Mattie and baby Samuel, goes on a strawberry-picking expedition with her neighbors. These are generous gestures that break the dam of debt behind which Dottie has been hiding. They suggest, very lightly, the possibility of grace. It is a chastened Dottie who sends Mattie away with her blessing, a grateful Dottie who lingers over the final two words of the postcard she receives, "Love, Mattie." And though we imagine that she will always be a woman who works hard and does her duty, we hear in the final pages of the novel a faint echo of Jesus' promise, "Consider the lilies of the field, how they grow; they neither toil nor spin; . . . But if God so clothes the grass of the field . . . will he not much more clothe you? . . . Therefore do not be anxious . . . " (Matthew 6:28, 30–31). As Dottie lies in bed one morning, "[w]ithout a thought of the day to come" (252), she looks in amazement at a flowering amaryllis Mattie gave to her before she left for California, a flower that grows in water, not earth—a flower as frivolous as braided hair or painted nails, as incomplete as a close-up photograph, as light as the breath of God.

The novel refuses, however, to tidy up Dottie's life. In the end, Dottie is left alone in her bedroom, and we are unsure how far her reconciliation with Mattie—and with God—will reach. Yet in the amaryllis—a gift she does not deserve or even understand, a flower that resists her efforts to care for it—we sense a quiet presence that lifts the heavy silence.

▣ Discussion Questions about the Novel

1. There are many kinds of silences in this novel, and not all of them are necessarily bad or even "heavy." What, for instance, do you make of Dottie's initial thought after Zela's death that if only Morris could sit with her at Mattie's bedside, they would wait quietly together "agreeing by our silence to give her a gift she would never know we had given" (9)? Is taciturnity a virtue, particularly in a small community where gossip is the coin of the realm?

2. Dottie makes much of the fact that she has no instinct for mothering. Her neighbor, George Hilliard, however, commenting on a ewe who rejects her own newborn lamb notes, "Life is more about choices than instinct." Could Dottie, given her personality and circumstances, have made different choices about the way she raised Mattie? Does she hide behind her lack of mothering instincts? Or do you think she has better instincts than either she or Mattie give her credit for?

3. Dottie's experiences of God throughout the novel are almost entirely negative. Yet she cannot quite give up her belief in him. Does she have a genuine faith that has been buried under hardship and disappointment, or is her belief merely the remnant of her childhood education? Does Stanley's steadfast love contribute to her spiritual awakening? Do you find Stanley's love for Dottie credible?

4. Few of us own a piece of land that we love as much as Dottie loved her farm. As we lose the tradition of passing down property from one generation to the next, do we lose something precious? Or does Dorothy's obsession warn us against the sentimentality of nostalgia?

5. When Dottie asks Stanley whether she should keep Mattie, he tells her to do what is right for the child and then adds, "You don't want her." Despite this advice, Dottie does keep Mattie, but does she do so for the right reasons? Is she fulfilling her friendship and implicit promises to Zela? Or is she making up for her own guilt in failing to realize the depth of Zela's despair? Does she genuinely want what is best for Mattie, or is she more motivated to keep Morris and Charlotte from having what they most want? Would it have been better for an artistic child like Mattie to have had a more compatible mother, like Charlotte, who might have encouraged her talents, or was the bracing atmosphere of hard work and farm life just what Mattie needed to grow into a strong and confident woman?

6. Dottie's spiritual and ethical life seems stunted by the ferocity with which she holds onto debts. To what extent is her own estrangement from God caused by her refusal to forgive others—a bitter reversal of Christ's promise to forgive our debts as we forgive our debtors?

■ **Other Books to Consider**

—Willa Cather, *My Ántonia*. Boston: Houghton Mifflin, 1918.

> As told by the narrator Jim Burden, the novel recounts the story of Ántonia Shimerda, a Bohemian peasant girl who has migrated with her family to the Nebraskan prairies, where she seems to become part of the land itself. For Jim and Ántonia, their meeting begins a deep and warm friendship that extends over many years, into his adult life and into the years of Ántonia's marriage; the novel ends with his peaceful sense that his life will always be enriched by the memories of this immigrant family and their valiant life on the prairies.

—Joyce Carol Oates, *We Were the Mulvaneys*. New York: Dutton, 1996.

> The Mulvaney clan seems to have all that makes life worth living; they are secure in their own family situation and in the rural community of which they are such an important part. But when the family is torn apart by an event that remains shrouded in silence, it will be decades before the youngest son, Judd, can unravel the story and bring the family back together in the joy that had once been their's.

—Jane Smiley, *1000 Acres*. New York: Knopf, 1991.

> In this retelling of Shakespeare's *King Lear*, Larry Cook, a proud farmer, decides to retire and turn over his farmland holdings to his daughters—two of whom receive the news gladly, the third suggesting it would be a bad idea, a suggestion that leads to her being disinherited. But as Ginny and Rose and their husbands set to work on their newly acquired land, Larry Cook transforms into something quite apart from the gentle retired farmer, and so the novel moves toward a divided family and an unstable world.

ROAD TO PERDITION

(1998)

Max Allan Collins
with art by Richard
Piers Rayner

Synopsis

When Michael O'Sullivan, Jr., recalls the winter of 1930, his memories are all in black and white, and so it is fitting that they be told in graphic novel form where simple words and black and white drawings come together to tell a story. But what starts as a seemingly innocent recollection of a childhood spent with a dedicated father, saintly mother, and beloved younger brother during the heady days of the gangland 1930s, quickly turns into a red-tinged tale of unmitigated violence and tragedy.

Michael O'Sullivan, the narrator's father, is the hired gun for John Looney, the Irish godfather of the Tri-Cities where the O'Sullivan family lives, and *Road to Perdition* unfolds as O'Sullivan's life as a mob assassin comes crashing into the life of his family. John Looney orders the death of O'Sullivan and his family because young Michael had tagged along on one of his father's "missions" and had witnessed the murder of a local bootlegger and his employees. O'Sullivan and his son escape the deaths ordered for them, but Annie and Peter O'Sullivan do not. The story of the novel emerges as O'Sullivan and his son travel across the Midwest, enacting vengeance and seeking sanctuary in a war of violence and betrayal that spirals out of control. In the end, even Michael O'Sullivan, the archangel of Death himself, cannot escape death at the hands of a mob killer, and only Michael, Jr. lives to tell their story and to remember his father in an act of both confession and absolution.

Max Allan Collins (b. 1948) first made a name for himself as a writer for the *Dick Tracy* comic strip; later, he wrote his Nathan Heller historical detective series (1983–2002). Growing up and living in the Tri-Cities area (Rock Island and Moline, Illinois, and Davenport, Iowa), Collins realized that the gangland dramas "had really happened, right where I lived"; that was the epiphany that inspired his career of "true crime" fiction and gangster *noir*. Indeed, most of Collins's fiction is set in the Midwest and features "real life" gangsters and mob figures; he has written books, comics, plays, and film screenplays in this genre.

After *Road to Perdition*, Collins wrote two sequels in traditional rather than graphic novel form, *Road to Purgatory* (2004) and *Road to Paradise* (2006), which continue the story of Michael O'Sullivan, Jr., through 1973. In these novels, Michael, Jr. has strangely returned to the world of mob violence and has become an enforcer, as his father had once been. In addition to these works, Collins is known for his novelizations and his books inspired by television shows such as *NYPD Blue*, *Bones*, and *Dark Angel* He has also written several screenplays.

Considering the Novel

Road to Perdition announces to the reader in its very title that it is a story of sin and salvation, right and wrong, justice and revenge. Yet it also suggests that things are not always as they seem and that life itself cannot be depicted in black and white.

It may seem an odd choice to include a graphic novel in a collection of traditional prose novels that explore questions of faith. But the graphic novel, with its interplay of words and images, makes us pay attention to the ways in which the stories we tell about ourselves and our families and our faith shape the ways we see the world. In traditional prose novels, it might be said that the words of the novel *tell* the story and any images or pictures are an add-on to *show* the story. But in *Road to Perdition*, as with any graphic novel, the images do more than show the story that the words tell. Rather, the words and images interact with each other, sometimes underscoring an important moment or moving the plot along, but more often making us stop to question what is really being said.

For instance, perdition is another name for hell—the place of total spiritual ruin in which the wicked must suffer and pay for their sins. Yet we soon learn that the town of Perdition, the destination of the narrator and his father, is an anticipated safe-haven. After the brutal murder of his wife and youngest son, O'Sullivan plans to take his surviving son to Perdition, Kansas, and seek sanctuary at the home of his brother-in-law. Thus the road to Perdition is simultaneously the road to heaven and longed-for peace, and the road to hell as O'Sullivan and his son enact their ever-bloodier retribution. An even greater irony develops as we notice that the pictures of the novel are drawn quite starkly in black and white. The novel repeatedly reminds us that things are not always simple, not often black and white, yet paradoxically the drawings present us only with black and white images.

As we begin the novel, we see a hand writing the opening lines of a memoir on a clean sheet of paper and read that "[m]y memories, like some people's dreams, are in black and white" (17). The next panel reports one of the narrator's memories: "I know we had summer, in the Tri-cities, but when I remember my childhood, it's always winter . . . snow and sludge and sleet mixed with dirt and cinders" (17). The image in this panel seems to illustrate these words by showing a dirty city street. However, this picture is not a realistic drawing, but rather a clever composite of black and white shapes (called negative and positive space or negative and positive values by graphic artists) that our eyes interpret as cars, telephone wires, snow, sludge, dirt, and cinders, streets and buildings. We reconstruct these black and white shapes as a complete image of a bleak city street, much as Michael, Jr., the narrator, reconstructs his childhood from his memories. We may even think that we see shades of gray in the picture, although Rayner, the artist, only creates the illusion of gray by drawing black lines very close together, a technique called cross-hatching.

The images of the story, then, work together with the verbal narrative. The hand writing the opening words of the novel suggests that the black and white themes of the story—sin and redemption, betrayal and retribution—will be shown in black and white, presenting the stark truth of what really happened. Yet, the city scene, drawn in black and white, appears gray. From its first pages, the novel promises to be a grim story about the loss of innocence and the impossibility of neatly parsing out justice from revenge, the impossibility of seeing things in black and white, but it is paradoxically committed to the page in starkly drawn black and white images.

One such black and white figure is Michael O'Sullivan, the narrator's father, clearly a larger-than-life character. He is described as "quiet," a "family man," and, to the narrator, the most honorable man he ever knew. A "proud veteran of the Great War," O'Sullivan appears to operate according to a strict moral code that values loyalty, duty, and family above all (22). However, O'Sullivan has another, darker side. He is also the enforcer of the local crime boss John Looney. Because of his exactitude, ferocity, and calm efficiency, O'Sullivan is known as the "archangel of Death" in the mob world, instantly recognizable and universally feared, the one who brings death at the bidding of a god-like Looney.

Nevertheless, O'Sullivan is not presented as a mere assassin or a simple ruthless killer. He may be the archangel of Death, but he becomes the archangel Michael. Christian tradition tells us that the archangel Michael fights against Satan, rescues the souls of the faithful (especially out of death), is the champion of God's people, and brings souls to judgment. O'Sullivan seems to take on these more heroic offices despite the narrator's claim that his father was no saint (171, 190).

After his betrayal of O'Sullivan, Looney and his son Connor become satanic enemies who must be brought to judgment and O'Sullivan is ultimately depicted as the champion of his murdered wife and son (290). This glorification of O'Sullivan is in part due to the fact that, save for the initial murders that Michael, Jr. sees his father commit, the rest of the killings in the novel are prompted by John Looney's betrayal of O'Sullivan, an act condemned even by the other gangland bosses (135, 246). As retribution for the murder of his innocent wife and son, the violence that O'Sullivan wreaks on those he holds responsible seems to be a matter of justice and of making the mobsters pay for their sins. Looney himself has given O'Sullivan this mandate to pursue justice when he tells O'Sullivan that "I will never ask you to employ your terrible talents on the innocent. Only the *disloyal*—or other soldiers, soldiers of my enemies—will be visited by my Michael, my archangel of Death . . . " (38). By his betrayal of O'Sullivan and his family, Looney loses his "innocence" and he and his other soldiers become appropriate targets for O'Sullivan's fury. O'Sullivan tells Michael, Jr., "[T]he fault is with the betrayers. Looney and his son. You are not responsible for the deaths of your mother and brother. And neither am I. But I *am* responsible for their retribution" (82). O'Sullivan's claim that he is responsible for making Looney and his son pay suggests that any murders he commits are justified by this "higher" purpose.

As the two of them travel through Illinois, Michael, Jr.'s father maintains a ritual of stopping at Catholic churches in order to "light a candle for the men he'd killed." He would "enter the confessional . . . I assume, to tell the priest of the sins he had just committed" (161). The ritual of confession that O'Sullivan observes suggests that he seeks and presumably receives absolution for his own sins after each murder. O'Sullivan explains that "[w]e're all sinners, son. That's the way we enter this world. But we can leave it forgiven" (190). The result is that O'Sullivan appears not as a man given over to murder and destruction but one bent on upholding the highest standards of justice. In this sense, O'Sullivan is again a terrible angel—an archangel of justice who is awesome and awful.

However, this depiction of O'Sullivan as a bringer of justice is not so clear-cut as it might first appear. The events are framed as Michael, Jr.'s own memory or confession of the events of his childhood—a memory that continually plays itself out in black and white, even though the events that happen are much more complicated. For instance, in the pages that depict Connor Looney confronting Gabel in the alley way (28–29), Rayner uses primarily thin lines and white space but renders the panels of the actual murders with much more black (32–35). In fact, our eye registers that the panels get blacker and blacker as the situation gets worse and worse, culminating in the revelation that Michael, Jr. has witnessed the entire event.

Nevertheless, even in this case (and others throughout the novel), in which the blackness of the images matches the blackness of the murders, the relationship between words and images is not simply transparent. For example, in the scene in which O'Sullivan kills the guards at Looney's house, he leaves his son in the car. This means, of course, that Michael, Jr. was not there to witness these acts, although they are displayed for us in the images on the page. In fact, the narrator explicitly rejects the opportunity to recount what he himself had experienced firsthand that night. Following the panel that depicts Looney's grand house, the image of the hand writing on clean paper reappears. We read that "I could recount the endless minutes I spent waiting in the car for my father; I could describe the terror of the sounds that did emanate from that house, from the cold blackness of that winter night. But instead I will depend on the writings of others . . . to reconstruct what must have happened when my father went looking for old man Looney" (85).

The narrator writes that he *could* tell us what he experienced but he won't. The panel of the hand writing is almost all white, suggesting a pause before the violence to come but also reminding us at this crucial juncture that the story is written after the fact. The next sequential panel is mostly black and depicts Michael, Jr. waiting with a gun in one hand and his father's watch in the other. It creates a sudden jolt back into the blackness of his memory of that night. What we see, then, is not an illustration of what "really happened," a showing of those events. Rather, Michael, Jr. has interpreted the accounts he read later and has constructed his own images—just as we construct the city street or the image of O'Sullivan creeping through the snowy darkness out of the black and white shapes on the page. Thus, the black images may match the black events described, but they are the events of memory and narrative and not a neutral depiction of what actually happened.

Of course, Michael, Jr. does not know "what actually happened" during any of the events recounted in this story. He tells us at the beginning of the novel that "[i]n retrospect, it's hard to imagine my father being part of any of that" (22), tells us that when he remembers the night his mother and brother were killed "it's at once vivid and a blur" (113), and tells us that all he really knows is "what rings true" about his father (171). Indeed, the repeated refrain that accompanies many of the more violent acts his father commits is "I can only imagine."

We should remember, too, that these are the memories of a boy who has experienced extreme trauma and has become an orphan by the novel's end. In the panel that depicts O'Sullivan walking down the hallway to Alexander Rance's office, Michael, Jr. claims his father is no butcher, but how can we believe that when we remember O'Sullivan carrying him down the stairs and out of a house that has become a scene of bloody carnage? This is also the scene in which Michael, Jr. kills a man. He says to his father, as they stand in a litter of corpses, "I don't want to go to hell, Papa" to which O'Sullivan responds, "*This* is hell, Michael" (187). O'Sullivan scoops him up to carry him out (188) and the second panel on the page depicts O'Sullivan kissing him on the cheek. This is a suddenly much younger-looking Michael, Jr. and the narrator says in the caption that "I'll also never forget the tenderness of how Papa carried me. When I was much smaller, he'd carried me up the stairs and to bed like this" (188). Is this the sudden inclusion of an even more distant memory? A memory of his father carrying him to bed instead of carrying him out of hell? The sequence concludes with a stark image of O'Sullivan getting into the car as Michael, Jr. sits behind the wheel. This time, Michael's face is older, hardened, and in the same black shadowing as his father.

Because this is Michael, Jr.'s memoir, because he was not present at most of these brutal scenes, because he is being changed and perhaps even wants to defend his father from the charge that he turned his own son into a killer, we cannot blindly trust the picture he paints for us of his father and his father's actions. We may be all too willing to excuse O'Sullivan's actions when confronted with the visual representations of his murdered wife and young son—we share in his wrath and the sense that someone must pay. Yet, this is a picture presented to us by a son wanting to absolve his father. As the bodies pile up, we are forced to admit that O'Sullivan's murders are indiscriminate and exceed any notion of retributive justice, of demanding only "an eye for an eye."

Even if we accept that O'Sullivan is an angel of justice or retribution, the fight against the enemy is ambiguous. He tells his son that what he does for a living "is not to be admired" (42), and while he claims that he has to work out of duty to provide for his wife and family, the narrator explains that they had "the nicest house of anybody we knew (except for Mr. Looney)" (24). Surely O'Sullivan wasn't required to provide a home to rival a mob boss? O'Sullivan also ensures his son's loss of innocence by making him an accomplice in his crime spree. By teaching him to drive, handing him a gun, and assigning him a vital role in his plan, O'Sullivan is himself the corrupting element of the kind that produced the death of his wife and youngest son and the eventual orphaning of his oldest son. After Michael, Jr. first witnesses his father at work, he says, "I don't *want* to be a soldier" (44) but eventually he admits, "But I did want to be like him. Yes, I had seen the reality of battle. I had taken a life. I had sinned. But hadn't I been forgiven by God? Didn't God forgive soldiers for the sins war made them commit? And my father was a courageous soldier. He was a violent man, but not cruel" (240).

Michael, Jr.'s understanding of sin and forgiveness as a matter of balancing a ledger sheet is a provocative one. It suggests that no sin is so great that it cannot be forgiven if properly justified and properly atoned. Strangely, it is none other than Al Capone, a figure only present in a newspaper clipping and a portrait (117, 132, 137, 228) until he surfaces to discuss the situation of O'Sullivan and Looney with Frank Nitti, who unwittingly makes one of the more important statements about sin and forgiveness in the novel. When Nitti says of O'Sullivan "the Looneys killed his wife and son, Al. He was a loyal soldier and they sold him out" (246), Capone replies, "Life ain't all balance sheets and ledger books, Frank" (246).

The novel's ability to raise such questions is due, in part, to our almost overfamiliarity with the content of the story. That is, we have so many mobster films to draw upon, *Road to Perdition* seems formulaic. After all, this story of mob violence, loyalty, duty, and betrayal can be easily located in movies like *The Untouchables* or in the criminal worlds of Mickey Spillane and Raymond Chandler. For example, it is inevitable that O'Sullivan would be betrayed at the hands of John Looney's psychopathic son and that the betrayal would compel O'Sullivan, an almost iconic representation of loyalty itself, to undertake the murder of not only Connor Looney but also John Looney and anyone else who stands in his way. It is also not surprising that the narrator's aunt and uncle would themselves be murdered and that O'Sullivan would eventually be killed as well.

Yet this adherence to the rules of the mobster novel makes us more attentive to the emotional core of the novel, the scene in which the narrator kills for the first time and is comforted by his father as they participate in confession. Although this scene shows O'Sullivan as Michael, Jr. wants us to remember him, the emotions are nevertheless true. Such simple and poignant moments—a father comforting a frightened child and teaching him the rudiments of faith in the face of horrific violence—speak of the strange state in which we all find ourselves living. The world is *not* black and white and even a formulaic crime story can represent moments of beauty and normalcy. In fact, the formulaic nature of the story itself can be read as providing the backdrop and context for these larger questions about the nature of innocence, the difference between vengeance and justice, the inevitability of corruption, and so forth. The world of the gangsters may exist in a kind of absolute world of black and white, balance sheets and ledger books, violence and perverted rules about justice, but *this* story of a father and his son asks us to think about how we come to live in a world of gray.

The novel ends with the final revelation that Michael, Jr. has grown up and become a priest. The hand that writes the story reappears on the penultimate page and writes, "And now I've told the story, finally, of the soldier who was my father and can only ask that you pray for his soul. And mine" (301). The preceding panel depicts the covers of two historical accounts of his father, one depicting him as "a fiend" and the other as "an avenging angel." The narrator writes that after reading such accounts he "knew one day [he'd] have to write the story of the man [he] had known . . . " (301). This statement suggests that the story has been a matter of setting the record straight.

But as we turn the page, we are suddenly brought to the present moment and the hands that have guided us through the story now close the book and the scene draws back to reveal the adult Michael, Jr. in a priest's robes. Another priest says, "Father—it's time. Time for confession" (302). While it is clear that Michael, Jr. has perhaps written his own confession and asked the reader to pray for his soul, the intertwining narrative of the words and images in these last panels also suggest that rather than setting the story straight, a task that has been revealed to be an impossibility, he is offering absolution to his own father, the archangel of death: "Father—it's time. Time for confession." Perhaps, then, the memoir represents Michael, Jr.'s own call to his father that it is time for confession.

If such a call for confession retroactively inspires the story, then Michael, Jr.'s record of his father's story becomes an act of forgiveness or absolution that *he* gives to his father. If it is, then the tenderness of Michael, Jr.'s act of absolution, in all its complexity and contradiction, his care for O'Sullivan's soul, and his desire to continue to bring forgiveness to those who have sinned, suggests that mercy and judgment will always be in tension in this world and can only be resolved in the world to come.

▣ Discussion Questions about the Novel

1. The title of the novel is *Road to Perdition*. Perdition for whom? Which characters are on the road to perdition? How does the meaning of "perdition" or the phrase "road to perdition" change throughout the novel? Is Michael O'Sullivan forgiven at the end of the novel? Does the narrator have anything he needs to seek forgiveness for? Is he a "son of perdition" or is he an innocent victim of the drama?

2. The novel is graphic in the sense that it is illustrated but it is also graphic in the sense that it is incredibly violent. What do you make of this depiction of violence? Is violence in this comic form meant to be beautiful? Is it meant to shock us? Is turning violence into a well-told and even beautiful story something that we, the readers, ought to be careful of? Is there a place for such things in a reader's diet?

3. What role does the church play in the novel? What do you make of the fact that Michael O'Sullivan insists on going to confession after every murder? Are these confessional scenes merely a ritual, or does O'Sullivan seem to be acutely aware of his own sin? Were you surprised to discover at the novel's end that the narrator has become a priest? Is religion presented in a positive or negative light in the novel?

4. What does the novel teach us about innocence? Are any characters truly innocent or are all fallen and in need of redemption? Does the world of the novel match your own understanding of what living in a fallen world looks like?

5. Because graphic novels present words and images in rhythmic interplay, they encourage us to think more explicitly about the nature of stories and telling stories. As a graphic novel moves by discrete steps from one panel to the next, each step that builds the story from beginning to middle to end calls attention to itself in ways that the mere words of a traditional story do not. Because we are aware of these steps, we are more likely to ask about how stories are put together. What elements need to be in place for a story to succeed? How do we define a successful story? Is it the words or the language of the author that makes a story what it is? Or is the role of the reader important? Is a picture really worth a thousand words? Or do pictures leave too much up to the imagination?

◼ Other Books to Consider

—Paul Auster, Paul Karasik, and D. Mazzucchellil, *City of Glass: The Graphic Novel*. New York: Picador, 2004.

> When a novelist is mistakenly identified as a detective, he nonetheless takes on the case of a father who has abused his son with sensory deprivation in order to discover the language of God.

—Will Eisner, *The Contract with God Trilogy*. New York: W.W. Norton, 2005.

> Published soon after Eisner's death, these three works focus on the history of a Jewish tenement neighborhood in the Bronx.

—Scott McCloud, *Understanding Comics: The Invisible Art.* New York: Harper, 1994.

The indispensable guide to the ways in which graphic novels and comics use visuals to create meaning.

—Marjane Satrapi, *Chicken with Plums.* New York: Pantheon, 2006.

When Nassar Ali han, the author's great-uncle and consummate Iranian musician, finds his beloved instrument broken, he goes to bed, because life is no longer worth living. While waiting to die, he is visited by his family, his memories, and hallucinations—and so eight days pass until his death.

—Marjane Satrapi, *Persepolis 1: The Story of a Childhood.* New York: Pantheon, 2004.

Marji tells the story of her life in Iran from the age of ten, following the Islamic Revolution and recounting the dangers of her independent spirit in the new fundamentalist regime.

—Marjane Satrapi, *Persepolis 2: The Story of a Return.* New York: Pantheon, 2005.

Freed from the religious extremism of Iran, Marji nonetheless discovers the danger of cultural freedom. She eventually returns to Iran and decides to live within the constraints of Islamic law, trying to find a balance between independence and religious dictates.

—Art Spiegelman, *Maus I: My Father Bleeds History.* New York: Pantheon, 1986. *Maus II: And Here My Troubles Began.* New York: Pantheon, 1991.

Winner of the 1992 Pulitzer Prize, this two-part story of a mouse, Artie, and his father Vladek, a Holocaust survivor, caught the attention of American readers by portraying a sensitive subject in graphic novel form.

Integrative Discussion Questions
for Part Two

1. In all three novels in Part Two, someone commits—or almost commits—a great wrong: Dottie uses Mattie's inheritance to save her family farm; the archangel murders for his gangster master; Etta Heine refuses to sell Kabuo's family the strawberry farm for which they have paid; and Ishmael Chambers nearly lets an innocent man go to his death. Despite differences, do you see any similarities in the ways these characters configure their own lives, harm others, and then seek to make things right?

2. Would you consider Stanley in *This Heavy Silence* to be a saintly character? What about Michael Sullivan, Sr. in *Road to Perdition* or Kabuo Miyamoto in *Snow Falling on Cedars*? What roles do they play in these books and, if they are not saintly, what accounts for the goodness they exhibit? Is that goodness counteracted by the flaws in their characters? Or is there a better way to account for the rights and the wrongs in their lives?

3. All three of these novels investigate the relationship between parents and children. To what extent are children shaped by the choices of their parents—a reminder of the promise that the Lord will visit the iniquity of the parents upon the children to the third and fourth generation but will show mercy unto thousands of those who love him and keep his commandments? Can children atone for the sins of their parents? Must they? Are they fated to replicate the shortcomings of their parents? Why are stories of parents and children so powerful in novels?

PART THREE

"Thou Hast
Taught Me to Say"

"Thou Hast
Taught Me to Say"

In her book, *The Writing Life*, Annie Dillard asks, What are we here for? She asks this question specifically of writers, but also of all human beings. What are we here for? The answer she gives is surprising: "*Propter chorum*, the monks say: for the sake of the choir." We speak, we write, we tell the story, we bear witness to what we know and to what we have seen and to what we hope for. We speak to the choir, and we are part of the choir. For the writer, this speaking is done through the medium of language. Writers create stories and tales and plays and poems and dramas and essays as a way of bearing witness.

But writers have wrestled with what it means for a character or narrator to tell a story, to bear witness to what he or she has seen. And here, ambiguity abounds. Are all things truly in the eye of the beholder? Can perceptions be true in an objective way, or are they always biased, so that the teller can only give us slanted versions of what might have happened? Does language itself become a problem when a teller recounts an event? Are there things that cannot be recounted at all in language? Can a witness be trusted? And if a witness cannot be trusted, then how can we ever get at the truth?

Leif Enger, Yann Martel, and Ian McEwan all present us with witnesses of astonishing events. Each of those witnesses has ambiguous feelings about telling what he or she has seen—but each tells the story anyway. Yet even as the stories are being told, we readers also sense the presence of the author behind the tale, nudging us, and asking, Do you think this is the way it went? Could it really be something else that is going on? What do you make of this?

PEACE LIKE A RIVER Leif Enger
(2001)

Synopsis

In small-town Minnesota, Jeremiah Land is a school janitor
with the power to perform miracles. His son Reuben, a
severe asthmatic, is saved from death while a newborn,
thanks to his father's petition and God's direct intervention.
Reuben has grown up with this story—as well as his own
witnessing of his heroic and gracious father's new miracles.
As an eleven-year-old, Reuben also has a second family hero:
his older brother, Davy, a coolly confident teenager. Their
sister, Swede, a precocious nine-year-old, outstrips both in
intelligence and creativity.

After a conflict erupts between the Lands and two high
school hoodlums, Davy decides to take justice into his own
hands and shoots his family's enemies. Instead of claiming
self-defense, he escapes from prison and heads west. Jeremiah
loses his job and takes his children on a trek to North
Dakota in search of Davy. All the while, Swede composes
epic cowboy poetry that reflects the family's troubles.
Andreeson, an FBI agent, pursues the Lands, believing that
they will lead him to Davy, but they miraculously escape
to find shelter at the home of Roxanna Crawley. While
staying at Roxanna's home, Reuben secretly meets up with
Davy, who has been living nearby in the Badlands with Jape
Waltzer, a demonic outlaw. Waltzer also shares his shack
with Sara, a girl whom he controls as a slave.

Realizing that Waltzer plans to kill Andreeson, Reuben
reveals the whereabouts of Waltzer's hideout to his father,

but the outlaw and his companions escape. Davy, in turn, also escapes from Waltzer, taking Sara along with him to Minnesota. Unknown to them both, a vengeful Waltzer follows and reappears at the Land's home, shooting both Jeremiah and Reuben while Davy flees. Dying, the two Lands are immediately reunited in a run through heaven to meet God. Jeremiah, however, sends Reuben back to earth, now miraculously cured of the asthma that has plagued him since birth. As an adult, Reuben marries Sara and enjoys a full life, occasionally meeting up with Davy, who lives as a lonely fugitive in Canada.

On the Author

Born in 1961, Leif Enger grew up in Osakis, Minnesota, where his parents taught at the local high school. He studied English at Moorhead State University and worked for sixteen years at Minnesota Public Radio as a journalist and producer. Enger began to write mystery novels with his brother Lin, then a student at the Iowa Writer's Workshop and now professor of creative writing at Moorhead. Using the penname L.L. Enger, the brothers published five novels (largely unsuccessful) centered on Gun Pedersen, a retired baseball player. After abandoning mystery novels, Leif Enger began *Peace Like a River* on his own. Over five years, he steadily read his work out loud to his wife and two boys, who contributed their comments and criticism. (Notably, his eldest son suffered from asthma at the time and his younger son suggested the cowboy character Sunny Sundown.) The novel was published in 2001, and with its national success, Enger quit his job in radio and began to write fiction full-time. He lives with his family on a farm near Aitkin, Minnesota.

▓ Considering the Novel

Leif Enger has stated that he considered calling his novel "The Battle Hymn of Reuben Land." The comment may sound tongue-in-cheek, but it underscores the spiritual combat framing the entire book. While the ending may provide a picture of heavenly and earthly serenity, the story itself runs on the legs provided by the age-old battle between good and evil, faith and self-sufficiency, innocence and guilt, and, ultimately, life and death. In this battle, Reuben meets with a varied assortment of heroes and villains who offer him different models for adulthood.

At first, Reuben's "battle" is one between his family and two young men. Israel Finch and Tommy Basca find Dolly, a high school cheerleader, alone in the girls' locker room. Fortunately, Jeremiah Land is on duty as janitor and he trounces the two before they can rape her. Davy Land—Dolly's boyfriend—would like to inflict a more severe punishment on the two troublemakers, despite Israel's threats to take revenge on the family. When Basca and Finch tar the Land's door and then abduct Swede, Davy takes matters into his own hands and smashes the windows and lights of Finch's car. Basca and Finch respond by breaking into the Lands' home. But Davy has brought them into a trap and shoots the two as they enter his room. Once this crime has been committed, the conflict turns into a courtroom battle in which Reuben plays a key role as a witness. Enger inverts the plot of *To Kill a Mockingbird*, with the Finch family acting as the defendant while Reuben, the Scout-like narrator, takes the stand. Confronted by the clever prosecutor, Reuben succumbs to vanity and a desire to show off what he knows about the killing. Too late he realizes that "[p]ride is the rope that God allows us all" (89). He condemns his own brother by revealing that the shooting was premeditated, recognizing just a beat too late what he has done. This incident begins a motif whereby

Reuben's narration often becomes a confession of his failure to defend his family.

Within the story of Davy's crime, however, Reuben offers a more important, miraculous narrative. First, as a newborn baby, Reuben's lungs are so congested that he cannot breathe for twelve minutes. But his father Jeremiah, guided by God, runs into the delivery room, snatches the baby from the doctor's hands, and tells his child: "Reuben Land, in the name of the living God I am telling you to breathe" (3). Lazarus-like, Reuben returns from the dead and—a second miracle—there is no brain damage. As an adult narrator, then, Reuben sees his narrative role in apostolic terms: he has been "preserved . . . in order to be a witness" (4) to his father's miracles and saving power.

Indeed, Jeremiah's miracles do resemble biblical accounts, but with a Midwest flair and setting. He walks not on water, but off a flatbed grain truck onto thin air (17). He multiplies chowder, not bread and fishes (47). When the school superintendent Chester Holgren fires him unjustly, Jeremiah responds by healing him not of leprosy but of a "bedeviled complexion" (79–80). His touch even heals a wounded saddle (48). While Jesus walked safely through a blinded crowd, Jeremiah drives unseen through towns guarded by state troopers (165). Like Jesus, Jeremiah can show righteous anger, appearing as a "luminous," avenging angel who drives Finch and Basca out of the girls' locker room (24). Yet Jeremiah, unaccountably, does not heal Reuben's asthma.

By contrast, Davy represents the archetypal lonesome cowboy, the solitary young man who solves problems with his guts and his gun. When the novel begins, the family is goose hunting. Davy jams his Winchester in his brother's hands, points him toward the flocking birds, and says, "Take him, Rube" (7). He offers frontier manhood to his sickly younger brother—the rube, the country bumpkin, who awkwardly hoists the gun and misses his shot. By contrast, Davy effortlessly kills his goose with a single shot. But Reuben's admiration for his brother begins to diminish when Davy kills Tommy Basca in cold blood: "For an instant my brother seemed very small—like a stranger seen at a clear distance" (50). By his murderous action, Davy has joined the camp of Basca and Finch. Now Reuben must decide which flawed hero he should follow, either his father (the miracle man who does not cure his asthma) or Davy (the outlaw who chooses exile over life with his family).

Enger adds another layer to Reuben's battle of family loyalties when midway through the action he introduces Martin Andreeson, the FBI agent in pursuit of the fleeing Davy. Reuben and his sister, Swede, are quick to view Andreeson, "the putrid fed," as their enemy. Even Jeremiah puts his loyalties with his fugitive son and declares to Andreeson prophetically, "[Y]ou and I will not speak again" (125). But Jeremiah is a failed prophet. When the agent catches up with the family and even threatens to harass the Lands' close friends for harboring Davy, Jeremiah openly acknowledges that the two men are enemies (160). Yet what sounds like a typical conflict between Western independence and federal meddling takes a sudden, unexpected turn when Andreeson arrives at Roxanna's home and seeks Jeremiah's aid. Thanks to his healing of superintendent Holgren, Jeremiah has acquired the reputation of a holy man who can help the FBI (203).

Jeremiah wrestles with God in prayer before he finally decides to help Andreeson find his son. Reuben is not pleased, and Jeremiah, recognizing Reuben's preference for Old Testament tales of the Lord slaying his enemies, is led to remind his younger son of Jesus' command to love their enemies—something, of course, neither Davy nor Reuben has been inclined to do. (Nor, in fact, is the reader.) Surprisingly, Jeremiah and Andreeson become fast, first-name friends as their search progresses (269). The situation has been reversed. The righteous Jeremiah is now helping the Fed find Davy, a bad Land, hiding in the Badlands.

In a bold authorial move, Enger adds two other new characters to the story, making Reuben's battle a more complicated choice between earthly versions of heaven and hell. At Roxanna's, the Lands enjoy a degree of family bliss and contentment they have never before experienced. She provides everyday miracles by filling the role of a caring spouse and mother with tales of Butch Cassidy for Swede, physical healing for Reuben, powerful romance for Jeremiah, and real nourishment for all. Reuben enjoys this world; however, he leads a double life, sneaking out to meet Davy, whom he spies as a lone rider on a ridge (205). Davy takes Reuben to his hideaway and his "compadre," Jape Waltzer.

If Reuben is the rube, Waltzer is the "jape," the trickster who beguiles the young man with his "rapscallion eyebrows" and humorous formality (227–29). In contrast to Jeremiah's command to breathe "in the name of the living God" (3), Waltzer tells Reuben, "Make up your mind and *breathe*" (236). Reuben is confronted with a choice: he can indeed follow Davy and Waltzer and make his own destiny. Or he can trust in God to provide his every breath. In a scene modeled after Peter's denial of Christ, Reuben denies his father's faith. Lost under Waltzer's command, the boy thanks the outlaw and not God for his meal. Reuben then caves in completely, conceding that he has found Davy not through God's guidance but "great luck." Instead of a rooster, a pig immediately squeals, and Waltzer roars "like the devil must at Christian cowardice" (234).

Reuben will finally repent, inform his father about Waltzer, and join a posse—a dream of the West complete with horses, Winchester rifles, and deputies. But from his perspective, this dream is a betrayal worthy of a "ratfink" and an "apostate" (276), who turns into a double-crossing ratfink by misleading the sheriff and causing injury to the rancher Lonnie Ford. Once again, Reuben's story of witness turns into a confession of faithless wrongdoing.

The novel could easily have ended with a Wild West gun battle on a fiery Badlands' landscape. Imagine Reuben caught between smoke, flames, and the shots and shouts of Andreeson, Waltzer, and Davy. Instead, we have a more modern shootout, with the psychotic Waltzer calmly waiting to gun down the Land family at their farm in Minnesota. Enger shows here his experience as a mystery writer. Instead of giving lengthy speeches or interior monologues, the action bristles as Waltzer shoots Jeremiah, and Reuben escapes Roxanna's grasp, runs to his father, and is shot. While Enger doesn't single out any particular interpretation, the shootout has clear parallels with other key episodes in the novel. First, by shooting two people, Waltzer provides a mirror image to Davy, the double murderer. The wages of violence is death, now in the Land family. Second, in choosing to help his injured father, Reuben reveals that his heart belongs not to Waltzer but to his father—and receives from God the Father a glimpse of perfect peace on both heaven and earth. He had given up on Jeremiah ever curing his asthma ("One thing I wasn't waiting for was a miracle" [292]) and is resigned to the situation ("Fair is whatever God wants to do" [294]). The miracle happens when Reuben gives up asking, but does not give up on faith. Jeremiah then fully plays out the Christ-like role his earlier miracles foreshadow. Through a "transaction" with God, he gives up his own life to send his son back to earth (310). Later, as an adult, Reuben enjoys the blessings of health and a serene family life, complete with spouse, kids, and cinnamon rolls; but there is no transaction for Davy, whose life as a fugitive in Canada seems immensely dull and lonely.

Enger makes no apologies for the overt Christian messages of his book, basing its title on the nineteenth-century hymn, "It

Is Well with My Soul" that begins "When peace, like a river." Indeed, the struggle between a devilish character (Waltzer) and a Christ-like figure (Jeremiah) reflects the hymn's text ("Though Satan should buffet, though trials should come, let this blest assurance control: that Christ has regarded my helpless estate, and has shed his own blood for my soul"). Chapter titles also allude to the hymn ("When Sorrows Like Sea Billows Roll" [70]) and to related Scripture texts ("The Substance of Things Hoped For" [129] from Hebrews 11:1, a definition of faith). Moreover, Jeremiah is distinctly otherworldly for a central character. After a tornado lifts him into the sky—making him literally otherwordly—he decides to give up his medical studies, having been "baptized by that tornado into a life of new ambitions" (55). His goal is not worldly success, but a deeper spiritual life tied to intense prayer and continual study of his frayed King James Bible: "[O]h, but he worked that book; he held to it like a rope ladder," Reuben remembers (103). Religious conversations between other characters are also common. For example, Davy asks Reuben, "You think God looks out for us?" and "You want Him to?" (43). Reuben later comments, "Davy wanted life to be something you did on your own; the whole idea of a protective fatherly God annoyed him" (56). Through characters like Davy and Jeremiah, the novel asks readers to consider how they surmount trials and troubles—through self-reliance or trust in a protecting God.

But Enger preaches this message about God without being preachy, thanks in large part to the narrator's humorous voice. Reuben addresses the reader directly from start to finish ("How you yowled" [1] and "Stay with me now" [300]). His speech reflects both playground-speak (Andreeson is "the king of pukes" [204]) and coffee conversation ("I'm sorry, but nope" [3]). At the same time, Enger slips in humorous lines that go beyond the perceptions of an eleven-year-old. When Israel Finch enters

Reuben and Davy's bedroom and the lights go on, he "stood in the door with his pathetic club like a primal man squinting at extinction" (49). The young neighbor boy, Raymond, resembles "a small, hot, talkative planet" (115). The school cafeteria workers prepare "the daily grotesque" (75). Reuben also offers folksy wisdom ("Yes, yes sir—routine is worry's sly assassin" [27]) and makes paragraphs of single lines ("The answer, it seems to me now, lies in the miracles" [3] and the repeating "Make of it what you will" [311]). In fact, Enger uses Reuben as a ventriloquist narrator, shifting effortlessly between the voice of an eleven-year-old and that of a humorous and perceptive adult.

Enger also avoids sermonizing by creating characters that are marked by their displays of quick wit. Roxanna first wins over Swede not through her hospitality, but through her repartee ("'My sympathies,' Dad said. 'Appreciated but gratuitous,'" replies Roxanna [177]). Even Waltzer is an accomplished wordsmith, quick on the verbal draw. When Reuben says his goal is to breathe, the outlaw comments, "His aspiration is respiration" (235). Sometimes the wit is involuntary, making the characters even more likeable. Davy warns Reuben that he must say "Mr. Waltzer" when addressing Jape, which he does even amidst the asthma attack Waltzer provokes: "'Shut up!' I gasped. 'Shut up and let me be!' It was all the air I had. I paid for some more and added, 'Mr. Waltzer'" (236). Humor leavens serious situations (here a young boy tormented by the devil incarnate) and lightens accounts of the supernatural. For instance, Reuben is on the way to the privy when he sees his father walk on air; so as not to disturb the miracle, Reuben does his business in a willow thicket (18). Moreover, the miracle of the endless chowder is set within the comic tensions over Tin Lurvy's disruptive and gluttonous visits (47). Finally, Jeremiah gets a taste of perfect peace when a trumpet-playing preacher slays him with the spirit (33). Reuben flees, however, to the church kitchen where he receives Edenic fruit from the fingers of the aptly named Bethany Orchard (30).

Sometimes such comedy can take on an ironic tone: "Dad's reluctance to leave, so far as I know, had little to do with Roxanna. It had more to do with Almighty God, who so far had issued no instructions about what to do next" (193). Some may find that such irony and humor undercut the novel's serious spiritual message. But in addition to enlivening the story, these moments suggest perhaps that faith and life's miracles carry their portion of humor. In fact, Enger presents heaven as a place where laughter will take the place of language (300).

Swede's cowboy poetry also offers a good share of comic relief. That comedy comes chiefly from the contrast between the poetry's epic form and its colloquial language:

But deep in the distance and churning up smoke,
Who are the riders come charging for broke? (258)

At the same time, Swede's poetry reflects the novel's serious intent. Sunny must battle "the devil called Valdez" (27). Swede may at first have "a soft spot for the bad guy, like every other writer since Milton" (35), but after Finch and Basca abduct her, she becomes less sympathetic to her villain. She is unable, however, to kill her own devilish creation. Reuben asks her "who's running the story anyway?" (69) and realizes only later that "Valdez was no invention" (101). Her fear foreshadows Waltzer and also the "devilish little man" who threatens Reuben in his asthma-laden dreams (183, 237). Of course, both devils deal in death. Swede trusts, however, that everything is "going to turn out okay" for Sunny, who will live in a "perfect valley" (259). In the same way, according to Roxanna's story, Butch Cassidy does not die in South America, but finds work as a windmill installer—both poem and story pointing to the peace Jeremiah and Reuben find at the novel's conclusion.

Alongside humor, Enger adds a violent, even surreal edge to his tale. In a manner reminiscent of Flannery O'Connor, we read how Waltzer cuts off his own fingers and then tells Sara to dispose of them: "She picked up the canceled digits and threw them sack and all in the crackling stove" (252). As for Andreeson, Waltzer "bludgeoned him and rolled his poor corpse into the lignite to hiss" (309). And Davy "lowered the barrel to the base of Tommy Basca's skull. . . . He showed no tremor. He fired. Tommy relaxed" (50). Hunters and the hunted fill the story. And their violence, like Enger's style in these passages, is calculated and cool—and for that reason, all the more shocking. Even the postcard-perfect ending has some disturbing shadows: "Jape Waltzer proved as uncatchable as Swede's own Valdez" (309). Reuben speculates about Waltzer's whereabouts: "Maybe he's even old and repentant. Anything is possible. I only know he is apart from us and that, as Mr. Stevenson wrote of Long John, we're pleased to be quit of him" (309). If Waltzer is "apart from us," the story shows his violence is part of our lives. Reuben and Jeremiah may win a battle, but the war between life and death is not over.

In addition to Waltzer, another loose end is Davy, who learns that "[e]xile has its hollow hours" (310). When Jeremiah takes leave of Reuben in heaven, he says, *Tell Davy* (304). Tell him what? Reuben's main duty as a witness is no doubt to fill Davy's hollow life with the promise of heaven. The brothers meet in Canada and Davy tells Reuben to "[b]reathe. . . . Let's see you breathe," a reminder of the command made by both Jeremiah and Waltzer. But when Reuben breathes deep, Davy still questions his brother's story of heaven and healing (310–11). As in the biblical parable of the rich man, neither Jeremiah (speaking from among the dead) nor Reuben (returned from the dead) can make their son and brother repent and begin his life anew. Davy is hard-hearted, damned to doubt and disbelief. Given that Reuben is unsuccessful "witnessing" to him, the novel may appear pessimistic about repentance, conversion, and faith. "Make of it what you will," Reuben says repeatedly. Make something or nothing is the implication. In itself, a miracle cannot *make* someone believe. In Reuben's words, a miracle does act like "the swing of a sword" (4), cutting between those who have ears to hear and those who don't. For Enger, real belief must begin with an openness to God and, as the hymn "It Is Well with My Soul" has it, the trust that one day it shall be possible that "faith shall be sight."

▨ Discussion Questions about the Novel

1. The most striking aspect of the novel is its presentation of miracles and heaven. While this presentation may be easily discounted as the unreliable memories of an impressionable eleven-year-old, Enger clearly wants the reader to reflect on faith and the supernatural. At the beginning of the story, Reuben makes this comment: "People fear miracles because they fear being changed—though ignoring them will change you also" (3). How does this comment apply to the story? Do miracles change reality, whether you believe them or not?

2. Why does Enger present a picture of heaven at the end of the novel? How is that portrayal tied to the rest of the book and the miracles it presents? Is anything missing from Enger's portrait of heaven?

3. The novel offers the spiritual comfort and familiarity of "a favorite hymn remembered" (182). Some critics have contended, however, that the novel is too nostalgic. For those of you old enough to have experienced it, does Enger present an accurate portrayal of the 1960s?

4. According to Swede, every western is a love story. Is *Peace Like a River* both a western and a love story?

5. Many of the names in this novel have obvious meanings (Jeremiah and Reuben Land, Jape Waltzer, Bethany Orchard). What do you think Swede's name comes from or represents?

▨ Other Books to Consider
—Kent Haruf, *Plainsong*. New York: Knopf, 1999.

> Set in the small town of Holt, Colorado, on the edge of the Colorado plains, this is a story of small-town life, where pregnant girls may be sent away from home and find a new home with gruff cattlemen, where Tom Guthrie is searching for love, and where a teacher, Maggie Jones, can make all of the characters intersect and so find grace—despite loss and hurt and anger and loneliness.

—Harper Lee, *To Kill a Mockingbird*. Philadelphia: Lippincott, 1960.

> This classic southern novel is defined by the voice of young Scout, who watches her father and brother battle hatred and racism in the 1930s, herself coming to new understandings about human nature, all under the gentle and strong guidance of Atticus Finch.

—W.O. Mitchell, *Who Has Seen the Wind*. Toronto: Macmillan of Canada, 1947.

> Young Brian lives on the Canadian plains, and the wind that moves over them seems to him to be the breath of God. In this powerful coming of age novel, Brian encounters hatred, prejudice, and weakness in a small town—but also finds within his family and in his own heart the strength to face the wind.

—Brady Udall, *The Miracle Life of Edgar Mint*. New York: Norton, 2001.

> When Edgar Mint is run over by a mailman and his head crushed, he is given up for dead by his mother—but he in fact survives. Saved, he is institutionalized in several homes, but finally recovers and enters a school for Indians, where he is brutalized. He is finally rescued by a Mormon family, but even here, he finds the past coming to threaten him. A novel about forgiveness and safety in a dangerous and unforgiving world, it is also a story about the menaces of the past and the choices of the present.

LIFE OF PI   Yann Martel
(2001)

Synopsis

During a chance encounter in a coffee house in India, the novel's Canadian narrator learns of Pi Patel and "a story that will make you believe in God." We read Pi's own firsthand account of his childhood in India and his later studies of zoology and religion in Canada. These studies grew out of his father's business, a zoo in Pondicherry, and Pi's early interest in religion. As a boy, he embraces Hinduism, Christianity, and Islam, exasperating his parents and spiritual mentors. When the political situation in India worsens during the 1970s, Pi's father decides to immigrate to Canada and boards not only his family but also the animals of his zoo on a Japanese cargo ship. The ship sinks and Pi is thrown to a lifeboat that will also harbor a zebra, a hyena, an orangutan, and a Bengal tiger named Richard Parker. Pi survives the sea, predatory animals, an attack by a survivor from another lifeboat, and even a carnivorous island made of algae. Pi and Richard Parker finally wash ashore in Mexico, ending a 227-day journey. When the Japanese officials investigating the shipwreck doubt his account, Pi offers a second story—one that does not include animals but rather his mother, a sailor, the ship's cook, and acts of murder and cannibalism. The official report that concludes the novel chooses the first version, saluting Pi's courage on a lifeboat in the company of a tiger.

Born in Spain (1963), Yann Martel grew up in various countries across the world as his parents pursued graduate studies and then careers in the Canadian foreign service. At the University of Trent (Peterborough, Ontario), he completed a degree in philosophy. Traveling widely and taking on odd jobs, Martel began writing at twenty-seven and in 1993 published his first book, *The Facts behind the Helsinki Roccamatios*, a collection of short stories. In 1996, he published his first novel, *Self*, a work dealing with sexual identity. The story's main character is an eighteen-year-old man who is transformed into a woman, only to become a man again in his 20s. After the novel received mixed reviews and poor sales, Martel began a new novel based on a premise taken from the Brazilian writer Moacyr Scliar, whose *Max and the Cats* (1981) describes a German refugee crossing the Atlantic with a jaguar in his lifeboat. The result of extensive research, *Life of Pi* appeared in 2001 and the following year won the prestigious Man Booker Prize for Fiction. Although the ties between *Life of Pi* and Sciliar's novel caused some controversy at first, Martel's book was hailed as an exceptionally original work and gained a worldwide audience. Yann Martel currently lives in Montreal.

Considering the Novel

A book about the experiences of a Greek letter? Of a mathematical symbol? *Life of Pi*, by its very title, risks turning off a potential reader. In the same way, it would be easy to be turned off by the fictional *author's note* that begins the novel. The use of italics and a separate pagination, along with thanks to helpful persons and organizations make it seem an unnecessary preliminary. But these initial pages present the novel's main themes of hunger, fiction, and faith. Born of the narrator's own hunger for material and critical success, the novel goes on to describe the hunger of a young man for God and his physical hunger as a castaway. At the same time, the *author's note* boldly sets out the novel's main goal, nothing less than the attempt to make the reader believe in God (x). Parallel to that goal is the consideration of a story's power. "That's what fiction is about, isn't it, the selective transforming of reality? The twisting of it to bring out its essence?" asks the narrator, while contemplating the best way to a "greater truth" (viii).

Such term-paper worthy questions would certainly ruin the novel from the start if it were not for Martel's superb sense and use of humor. Before going to India to seek inspiration for a new novel, the narrator's sole preparation is to learn the word "bamboozle." When his writing project fails, he sends the book manuscript off to Siberia. And when an elderly man offers "a story that will make you believe in God," the narrator asks, "Does your story take place two thousand years ago in a remote corner of the Roman Empire?" (x). This comeback—and the story the book unfolds—are almost too good to be true. And isn't that what Martel is warning us from the start? We must take the story seriously, but not as religious nonfiction—for the book's full title is indeed *Life of Pi: a Novel*.

Parallels do exist between the narrator's life and Martel's—for example, they publish a mediocre novel in 1996 and also travel abroad. But did Martel really send a failed book manuscript to a "fictitious address in Siberia" (ix)? Martel voluntarily blurs the lines between his own life and the presentation of a *fictitious* narrator to raise questions about the nature of truth. In that regard, did Martel really meet Pi Patel in Toronto? Or is the novel a "selective transforming of reality" that hopes to bamboozle us into believing in God?

It may be useful to view the novel as a philosophical tall tale, an essay told not with footnotes, but intriguing characters and humor. In a marvelous twist of our expectations, the main character is neither a Greek letter nor a mathematical symbol but an East Indian with a curious name, "Piscine Molitor Patel." On one level, the origin of his name creates great comedy: a middle-class family in Pondicherry decides to honor a friend by naming their second son after his favorite swimming pool in Paris, the Molitor. The young "Molitor Swimming Pool" must endure childhood taunts, aided by the rude sound in English of the French word "piscine." Quite wisely, he shortens his name to "Pi" and imposes this change on every new teacher by writing his new name on the board, along with "$\pi = 3.14$" and a diagram of a circle and its diameter (23). On another level, this comic episode carries various symbolic connotations. "Piscine" points to a body of water in its contained and domesticated form. His new name "Pi" suggests at once the circular and the infinite. Pi compares this transformation to the spiritual name changes experienced by biblical characters like Saul/Paul (20). But it is Pi who baptizes himself through the trick of writing out his name on the chalkboard (23). And in that "irrational number with which scientists try to understand the universe" Pi finds "refuge" (24).

While such religious discussions and philosophical overtones fill the novel's first section, the spiritual message Martel offers is not exactly new. When his mother objects to his desire to be at once a Muslim and a Christian, the young Pi asks, "If there's only one nation in the sky, shouldn't all passports be valid for it?" (74). Contrary to fundamentalists of all religions, Pi feels we should not limit God to one specific religion or to our personal experience (49). His adult home in Toronto resembles a temple, or rather a warehouse, of religious signs and symbols ranging from a statue of Shiva to an image of Christ on the cross and a prayer rug (45–46). Pi displays a tolerance of other religions born not of indifference but amalgamation since all point to God.

Again, humor saves this message from sounding unoriginal. Pi's religious mentors, his "three wise men"—the pandit, imam, and priest—cross paths and argue: "But [Pi] can't be a Hindu, a Christian *and* a Muslim. It's impossible. He must choose" (69). Calling upon Gandhi as his model, Pi states his simple objective: "I just want to love God" (69). His father, the secular, modern Indian, deflects this crisis of faith with a snack: "That was my introduction to interfaith dialogue. Father bought three ice cream sandwiches" (70). In a similar amusing fashion, Pi tells of the encounter between his atheist school teacher and his Sufi mentor, both named Kumar, and both astonished by the grandeur of a zebra: a marvel of science for one, a glorious creature of God for the other. If Pi appreciates his school teacher, it is precisely for his living faith in science. What Pi rejects is agnosticism: "To choose doubt as a philosophy of life is akin to choosing immobility as a means of transportation" (28). In other words, agnosticism represents a passport to nowhere.

While the religious content of the novel finds depth through humor, the detailed descriptions of animal behavior represent perhaps the most surprising and engaging aspect of Martel's writing. In the first section, he draws us into a consideration of topics ranging from the three-toed sloth to an animal's sense of territory, the concept of flight distance, and the training of alpha and omega animals. The discussion of animals, however, is usually framed in religious terms. Pi remembers the family zoo as "paradise on earth" (14). Addressing those who criticize zoos, he notes: "I know zoos are no longer in people's good graces. Religion faces the same problem. Certain illusions about freedom plague them both" (19). A zoo is a place where animals and humans can relax. This peace is usually broken by those who see animals through "human eyes": "The obsession with putting ourselves at the centre of everything is the bane not only of theologians but also of zoologists" (31). In a zoo, this means some humans will forget that a wild bear is not a teddy bear or will mistreat an animal out of a mixture of sadism and stupidity. But why does Martel draw the parallel between zoos and religion? Is religion ideally a cage that allows humans to live at peace, and perhaps look at each other now and then (19)?

The novel may be philosophy and religion expressed through zoology, yet it can also boast the narrative strengths of any best-selling page-turner. First, Martel knows how to arouse our curiosity. Who is Richard Parker, a man (a lover?) who abandoned Pi (6)? Why does Richard Parker figure in the family photo album (87)? Martel also likes to catch the reader off guard through the use of rapid transitions. When the narrator describes Pi's children in Toronto at the end of the novel's first section, we are assured, "This story has a happy ending" (93). Turn a few pages, and the next section begins: "The ship sank" (97). We wonder how a teenage boy could ever survive the Pacific. In itself, this situation would qualify as material for an adventure story, but Martel adds a few complications. A mini-zoo of animal survivors joins Pi on a lifeboat to create no small amount of suspense.

But stated in plain terms, the story's premise is preposterous: a tiger and a boy, on a lifeboat? If Martel can stretch Pi's survival tale over some 200 gripping pages, it's thanks to the amount of credible detail he provides about the situation. Indeed, the novel is no sweet fantasy with cute critters. While his tone is usually light and amusing, Martel offers some extremely gruesome passages, enough to turn the stomach of any animal lover. Already in the first section, he prepares the reader for such violence when Pi's father makes his sons watch a tiger kill a panic-stricken goat. The attack is not described but the sound is enough to scare "the living vegetarian daylights" out of Pi (36). On the lifeboat, the hyena rips off a leg from the zebra and then eats it alive—from the inside of its belly (120, 125). Orange Juice, the magnificent orangutan, loses a valiant fight with the hyena and is beheaded (132). Richard Parker kills the survivor from another lifeboat: "He ripped the flesh off the man's frame and cracked his bones" (255). The smell of blood fills Pi's nose and ours. As in a well-done horror movie, such gruesome images play to our deepest fears and also mask the improbability of the horrific situation.

Life of Pi may have some of the characteristics of a thriller, but it is really a survivor's tale, engaging the reader through Pi's ingenuity and courage in the face of improbable odds. Think of how Pi constructs a raft or of his difficulties with fishing and water collection, not to forget the taming of a 450-pound Bengal tiger. In fact, the tiger gives order and purpose to his days. Instead of drowning in depression, Pi makes a life for himself, built on the rituals of prayer, food preparation, and animal taming. The calm sense of honest work—of tending and keeping—is astonishing amid the scenes of gruesome violence.

A reader may find that Martel has filled the lifeboat a bit too full. Could a space of one hundred and twenty square feet (imagine an average-sized bedroom, but narrowed to five feet by twenty feet) hold a Bengal tiger, a zebra, a hyena, an orangutan, and a boy, along with oars and lifejackets (138)? How could that boy tame a tiger, armed with a whistle and a tortoise shell as a shield? There are other possible tipping points, such as the conversation between the blinded Pi and another blinded survivor on the topic of French cuisine. (In mentioning traditional dishes such as tripes and brain soufflé, the French-Canadian Martel is probably indulging in a fun poke at the offal side of French cuisine [244–45].) And in what represents the longest stretch of our imaginations, Pi asks us to believe in his stay on a spectacular algae island that hosts a million meerkats and a man-eating tree. As the story expands in its imaginative scope, Pi counters disbelief with the proof of Pi: he speaks, therefore the story is true (223).

Humor, violence, survival skills, and fantasy: does that make you believe in God? After the lengthy descriptions of Christianity, Islam, and Hinduism in the first section, the novel avoids dwelling on any of these religious in the second section. On the lifeboat, Pi piously observes all the rituals he knows, but does he offer any highly developed reflection on who God is or perhaps should be?

Nonetheless, religious references continue to abound in the second section. Orange Juice arrives "floating on an island of bananas in a halo of light, as lovely as the Virgin Mary" (111); in death "[s]he looked like a simian Christ on the Cross" (132). After the wreck, Pi realizes, "A tiger aboard and I had waited three days and three nights to save my life!" (150). In addition to these references to Christianity, the lifeboat is described as being orange, which Pi identifies as a Hindu color (138). The algae island is green, the color of Islam (257), and the meerkats, as they eat the algae, remind Pi of prayer time at a mosque (266). In that context, it might be possible to pick apart the novel according to location, color, and religion. (The lifeboat would be Hinduism, the island Islam, and the blue sky and sea, Christianity.) But the very orange orangutan is compared not to Hindi deities but to Mary and Christ. And just as Pi cries out to "Jesus, Mary, Muhammad and Vishnu" (97, 150), Martel seems most interested in mixing religions, and so mixing religious symbolism. Pi leaves the paradise of Zootown in Pondicherry to find himself in a *life*-boat, an ark set adrift and ruled by the law of the jungle. In the boat, Pi confronts "the reality of Richard Parker," the reality of his own death (147). As he learns to tame the tiger, he learns to tame his fear of death and regains a sense of paradise.

Given the alternate ending in the final section, some may feel the book argues that reality and truth are of our own making. As Pi asks at the end of the novel: "The world isn't just the way it is. It is how we understand it, no?" (302). Such a reading, however, misses the moral battle at the heart of Pi's survivor-salvation story. When the zebra suffers the hyena's attacks, Pi does nothing, choosing to save his own skin (120). And the boy who at first bemoans the killing of a fish steadily begins to eat, sleep, and hunt like an animal (225, 231, 239). While he doesn't eat the man that Richard Parker kills, Pi uses human flesh as bait (256). When Pi steps on the mysterious algae island, he shouts, "Richard Parker! Land! Land! We are saved!" (258). But the island turns into another inverted Eden, offering only a bitter fruit: "a lonely half-life of physical comfort and spiritual death" (283). In other words, a life of selfishness that will consume a person slowly, teeth and all.

A paragraph taken from the narrator's notes on a conversation with Pi in Toronto highlights this message. The narrator is tired of his own "glum contentment" and gives a character sketch of Pi: "Words of divine consciousness: moral exaltation; lasting feelings of elevation, elation, joy; a quickening of the moral sense, which strikes one as more important than an intellectual understanding of things; an alignment of the universe along moral lines, not intellectual ones; a realization that the founding principle of existence is what we call love, which works itself out sometimes not clearly, not cleanly, not immediately, nonetheless ineluctably." The narrator then wonders about God's silence and decides to add—in conclusion—about Pi: "[a]n intellect confounded yet a trusting sense of presence and of ultimate purpose" (63).

It may seem as though God is absent from Pi's survival story. By his own ingenuity, Pi succeeds in finding food, water, and safety from a deadly tiger. Yet, a rat suddenly appears, jumps on Pi's head, and provides him with the initial offering needed to tame Richard Parker (152). In the same way, flying fish land right at Pi's feet when he needs bait (180–81). And the boat finally drifts to the coast of Mexico (284). The word is never mentioned, but doesn't this sound a lot like providence? Note how Pi prays when he realizes how close he is to death: "Now I will turn miracle into routine. The amazing will be seen every day. I will put in all the hard work necessary. Yes, so long as God is with me, I will not die. Amen" (148). In trusting that God will provide, Pi finds "peace, purpose . . . even wholeness" (162).

Pi's conversation with the Japanese investigators, Mr. Chiba and Mr. Okamoto, serves to illustrate a major obstacle to such faith. When Pi justifies his taming of a tiger, they exclaim: "In a *lifeboat*? Come on, Mr. Patel, it's too hard to believe!" (297). Pi then offers a second story that confirms their vision of reality (302). In this reality, if stranded on a lifeboat, a cook might indeed cannibalize a sailor and a boy's mother, and the boy might kill the cook in revenge. Such violence belongs not to animals but to human monsters (307–8). And as opposed to the "crude reality" (xii) we hear about each day in the news, isn't the "better story" one in which a boy learns to love his neighbor, a tiger? Wouldn't such love prey on your mind and make you hunger for something more in life—someone called God?

Alongside his faith, Pi also demonstrates an incredible sense of hope, joy, and wonderment. There is the joy of humor in the face of disaster. When Orange Juice arrives on a net of bananas, the net breaks: "It was a banana split in the wrong sense of the term" (112). And there is the joy of language ("[b]y dint of dinting" Pi opens a can [142]) and the comedy found even in the advice of a survival manual ("Always read instructions carefully" it begins, and ends with "Good luck!" [166–67]). Throughout his ordeal, Pi continues to hope (159,

176) and find God (209). Even as he faces certain death in an ocean thunderstorm, his eyes open to God's grandeur and he finds happiness (233). And if we view our life's story through reason alone, we risk not only missing God's love but also a great measure of joy, comedy, hope, and grandeur.

▨ Discussion Questions about the Novel

1. Martel uses a novel to justify belief in God, but does his method of offering alternative versions of the same story undercut his goal? What image of God did you come away with, after reading this novel?

2. "Piscine (Pi) Molitor Patel" is a name that creates a great deal of comedy ranging from potty humor to bleak irony (a swimming pool trapped in a lifeboat!). At the same time, "Pi" allows Martel to point to notions of transcendence. What does your name mean? Has your name (first, last, or nickname) shaped your identity in any way, in how you view yourself or in how others have treated or treat you?

3. In *Life of Pi*, violent, animalistic human behavior is contrasted to a life bound to faith in God. Does Martel then divide life between two opposing options, the animal and spiritual? If so, what does it mean to be human?

4. In criticizing a view of life based on "dry, yeastless factuality" (302), does *Life of Pi* reject science? If not, do science and faith in God live together in Martel's novel? Or are they like a tiger and a boy on a boat, the one having to either eat or tame the other?

5. Pi asks that his story be told in one hundred chapters because he dislikes his nickname and "the way that number runs on forever. It's important in life to conclude things properly" (285). Does the novel conclude properly? Or given its alternate ending, is it really a never-ending, circular work?

6. In the first chapter, Pi indicates he studied at university the three-toed sloth—of which we learn quite a bit. He also notes he wrote a fourth-year thesis on the "cosmogony theory of Isaac Luria, the great sixteenth-century Kabbalist" (3). Yet the novel does not discuss Luria (1534–72) in any detail, nor his idea of *tsimtsum*—that God retreated to make space for the created world. But the word is used on numerous occasions to identify what (large, sinking, Japanese) object? What significance might this have for the novel?

▪ Other Books to Consider

—Kate DiCamillo, *The Tale of Despereaux*. Cambridge, MA: Candlewick Press, 2003.

> A tale of courage, betrayal, and trust among mice and humans in a fantasy whose characters search for the light that the narrator holds out for them.

—Rohinton Mistry, *A Fine Balance*. New York: Vintage, 1995.

> In 1975, during a constitutional crisis in India, four people from India's working poor struggle to survive in a country whose failing government is marked by corruption.

—Salman Rushdie, *Midnight's Children*. New York: Knopf, 1980.

> Two children, born at midnight on the night of India's inpendence in 1947, are mistakenly exchanged, and so the son of a wealthy

Muslim family is sent to live in a Hindu tenement. Saleem, the Hindu child sent to live in wealth, has magical powers—like all those born on this midnight—and is able to discern his true birth, leading to enormous difficulties that are set against the backdrop of India's early years of independence.

—Louis Sachar, *Holes*. New York: Farrar, Straus, 1998.

In this dual narrative of survival, Stanley tries to survive his imprisonment in a camp in the deserts of Texas, in which he is caught up in a larger story that spans generations.

—François Marie Arouet de Voltaire, *Candide*. London: J. Nourse, 1759.

An adventure story in which Candide is forced to place the optimistic philosophy, that this is the best of all possible worlds, against his experience in the real world. The resulting clash of the two results in his rejection of optimism, and his assertion that we should all go out to tend our own gardens.

ATONEMENT Ian McEwan
(2001)

Synopsis

Atonement begins in 1935, and recounts the events of one
weekend at the home of the Tallis family who live near
London. When thirteen-year-old Briony Tallis witnesses
an encounter between her older sister, Cecilia, and
Robbie Turner, the son of the Tallis's housekeeper, she
misinterprets their awkward flirtation. Her misperception
escalates into a confrontation that shatters the entire
family when she accuses Robbie of raping their cousin.
The novel continues after a hiatus of five years as a
disgraced Robbie, now a foot soldier, treks across France
toward Dunkirk in the late spring of 1940. Meanwhile
Briony, an eighteen-year-old nurse probationer in London,
cares for wounded soldiers and seeks reconciliation with
her family. The novel concludes with Briony's reflections
on her life on the occasion of her seventy-seventh birthday.

Although McEwan focuses on Briony's moral and
intellectual development, he also takes us inside the
thoughts and motivations of many of the other characters.
He deftly explores how little we understand not only other
people, but also our own desires and actions, and how
easily we rationalize our own blind rush to judgment.

On the Author

Ian McEwan (b. 1948) was born in England but, as the son
of an army officer, spent much of his childhood overseas. He
graduated from Sussex University and later finished an MA
in creative writing from the University of East Anglia. His
first collection of short stories, *First Love, Last Rites* (1975),

won the Somerset Maugham Award; many of his subsequent works have also won awards, including the Whitbread Novel Award for both *The Child in Time* (1987) and *Atonement*, the Booker Prize for *Amsterdam* (1998), and the James Tait Black Memorial Prize for *Saturday* (2005). Atonement has recently been made into an award-winning motion picture

McEwan's works are known for their carefully designed plots, acute psychological and social insights, and beautifully crafted sentences. In addition to a dozen novels and numerous short stories, he has also written plays, film scripts, a children's book, and *Or Shall We Die?* the libretto for an oratorio.

■ Considering the Novel

Atonement the novel begins and ends with a play. It is not a very good play, but thirteen-year-old Briony (BREE-ah-nee) Tallis pours all her energy into it during "a two-day tempest of composition" (3). Briony's masterpiece, *The Trials of Arabella*, follows its heroine through her reckless passion for a wicked foreign count, to a bout with cholera and abandonment by lover, friends, and family, to Arabella's final restoration to health and happiness by a kindly prince disguised as a doctor. *The Trials of Arabella* appears again at the end of novel, which concludes with a description of its first performance on the occasion of Briony's seventy-seventh birthday. It is no accident that McEwan frames his book, and the intervening sixty-four years, with this childish romance. At its most basic level, *The Trials of Arabella* is a morality play in three acts—sin, punishment, and redemption— and at *its* most basic level, *Atonement* tells a similar story.

The novel begins quietly, innocently—as crime stories often do—and, in the tradition of classic English murder mysteries, it is set in a country home during a long hot weekend in the summer of 1935. The cast appears to be a rather ordinary family: Briony, her parents Jack and Emily Tallis, and her older siblings, Leon and Cecilia. But we are soon made aware of the tensions and frustration that simmer just below the surface. Jack, the father, who works in London, is seldom at home; in fact, he never actually makes an appearance in the entire novel. Though he claims to spend his late nights at the office, both we and his wife know differently. Emily, the mother, spends much of her time in bed, prostrate with migraines. Although she loves her family, she is nearly as distant as her husband, able to embrace her children only in the most whispery—and largely ineffective—way, with "a tentacular awareness that reached out from the dimness and moved through the house, unseen, and all-knowing" (63). Cecilia, newly graduated from Cambridge, is at loose ends as she contemplates what she should do with her life. She alternates between trying to manage the house in the virtual absence of her mother and lying on her bed reading fat eighteenth-century novels. Leon, the older brother for whom Briony has written *The Trials of Arabella*, breezes down from London, bringing with him an acquaintance, Paul Marshall, whom Cecilia characterizes as "nearly handsome, hugely rich, and unfathomably stupid" (47). Four more outsiders complete the cast: Robbie Turner, son of the Tallis's longtime housekeeper, and the Quincey cousins—fifteen-year-old Lola and the nine-year-old twins, Jackson and Pierrot—children of Emily's sister and refugees from a bitter divorce.

The impending disaster that eventually engulfs the Tallis family builds from two directions and is precipitated in both cases by the outsiders. Although Briony is excited that the arrival of the Quincey children means she will have actors for her play, she soon realizes that she cannot control real people as easily as her characters on the page. Lola calmly hijacks the role of leading lady, the twins turn every line of poetry into deadly prose, Briony finds herself sidelined in her own production, and Paul Marshall, who has no assigned role in the play, turns up in the old nursery rehearsal room with uncomfortable frequency.

The second disruption is caused by Robbie Turner, who, like Cecilia, has just graduated from university. Unlike Cecilia, however, Robbie knows exactly what he wants: he wants to become a doctor and he wants Cecilia, who has been deliberately (and provocatively) ignoring him of late. Both desires intertwine as he doodles his way through *Gray's Anatomy*, alternatively dreaming of practicing medicine and loving Cecilia. With this sexual tension in the hot summer air, it is no surprise that Robbie and Cecilia bumble into an awkward encounter. As Cecilia fills an antique Meissen vase from a fountain in the garden, Robbie arrives to help. He grabs the vase, she tugs back, the vase breaks, and two pieces fall into the pool. Whereupon Cecilia strips to her underwear, dives into the pool, recovers the porcelain shards, and stalks back to the house, leaving an open-mouthed Robbie in her wake. Briony, who has witnessed the scene from a distance, gapes from an upstairs window.

In and of itself, the encounter at the fountain is a tiny event, a bit of flotsam in the stream of time, trivial and easily dismissed. It assumes significance only as the Tallis sisters and Robbie try to make sense of it by telling themselves stories that set the incident into the larger pattern of their lives. Cecilia worries that she has looked even stupider than usual in front of the childhood friend who has grown into a handsome stranger; Robbie is drawn more deeply into love and lust by the vision of the "frail white nymph" rising out of the water (29); and Briony, fresh from the perils of Arabella, is frightened by a pantomime she cannot understand. To her eye, it appears that her sister is in danger: that Robbie has commanded Cecilia to undress and that Cecilia, shivering and unwilling, has done his bidding.

From this point on, McEwan edges his domestic story closer to the plot of a Shakespearean tragedy. He includes a Romeo and Juliet love that crisscrosses family and class lines; mis-written, mis-sent, and mis-read letters; a play within a play; a hidden villain; runaway twins; a sexual assault; and finally a false accusation. McEwan allows us, as readers, to see these events from several different perspectives. We sit with Robbie in his bedroom as he writes love letters to Cecilia, and we sense their mutual passion when they encounter each other later in the library. We mistrust Paul Marshall and his clever plan to market his Amo candy bar to the British army and his trips up to the old nursery. We worry that Lola's sexual awakening is turning her into a Lolita.

Although we are able to understand these events as adults, Briony is at a distinct disadvantage. Her perspective, and therefore her storytelling, is limited by her own inexperience and by her commitment to Arabella's rigid sexual and moral code: if you fall in love you get married and then you kiss; if you act recklessly and wickedly, you are punished. When Lola appears with badly chafed wrists and bruised arms, Briony cannot quite accept the explanation that the twins have injured their sister in an overly robust sibling brawl, but neither can she imagine what has actually happened. When she reads Robbie's sexually explicit letter to Cecilia or sees her sister kissing Robbie in the library, she cannot understand their love for each other, but she can understand her own horror and repulsion. So when she finds the dazed Lola rocking herself on a grassy bank after a sexual assault, she converts her confusion and horror and moral certainty into a coherent—but untrue—story in which Lola and Cecilia become the misguided Arabellas, Robbie the wicked foreign count, and she herself the avenging, princely doctor who restores the family to its prefallen state. This is a story she can understand, and this is the story she tells, a story which becomes the lie which becomes the accusation that sends Robbie Turner to Wandsworth Prison.

Part One concludes with a self-satisfied and thoroughly deluded Briony, basking in her role as Cecilia's savior, in her confidence that "this tragedy was bound to bring them closer" (173). As we can guess and as the novel later confirms, Robbie's arrest for the rape of Lola does not bring the sisters closer but rather causes a breach between Cecilia and Briony—indeed between Cecilia and her entire family—that is complete and irreparable.

McEwan, however, does not linger on Briony's inevitable shock as the repercussions of her storytelling begin to dawn upon her. Instead, he opens Part Two with an abrupt change of scene and point of view: "There were horrors enough, but it was the unexpected detail that threw him and afterward would not let him go" (179). Within a page or two, we realize that the "horrors" are those of World War II and the "him" is Robbie himself. It is May 1940 and British troops are dragging their way across France towards Dunkirk. Robbie Turner is among them, his prison sentence commuted into service as a foot soldier. He has experienced horrors as a prisoner and horrors as a soldier, but the unexpected detail that arrests his attention is a single leg dangling from a tree, "a perfect leg, pale, smooth, small enough to be a child's" (180). McEwan doesn't tell us why this leg unnerves Robbie. Is its very ordinariness a reminder of home and all that he has lost? Does its smallness evoke a memory of Briony and her inexplicable betrayal? Might its surreal presence symbolize all the displacement and isolation he has experienced? Perhaps these and more.

For some readers, Part Two is the most moving section of the novel and not simply because it paints a poignant picture of ordinary soldiers and civilians caught up in the horrors of war.

What we remember as we plod along with Robbie in his harrowing trek toward Dunkirk is that not so long ago Robbie imagined himself on a far different journey—toward medical school, a successful practice, marriage with Cecilia, a family of his own. Now the march across France unspools as a dreadful parody of that journey: the drawings in *Gray's Anatomy* come to nightmarish life as body parts strewn across the countryside; the would-be doctor cannot stanch his own wound; despite his best efforts, he cannot protect a Flemish child; and Cecilia has withdrawn into a haunting memory and a voice, "I'll wait for you. Come back," that draws him toward the sea and England. As readers, we too are haunted by the echoes of war we now recall from Part One— the "sodden tea towels" in the Tallis kitchen, "tributes to heroic forgotten labors, [which] drooped above the range like decaying regimental banners in church" (98) or the infamous Meissen vase, itself a talisman from World War I and now an emblem of all that has gone so terribly wrong. What we mourn is not just Robbie's misfortune, but all the lost hopes and dreams of all the soldiers in all the futile wars that have ever been fought. But Robbie's ordeal is also particularly his own and, within the scope of the novel's plot, it has become part of the punishment that is meted out for his "crime"; or perhaps better, it has become the ordeal Robbie must suffer as a consequence of Briony's crime.

Part Three returns us to England and to Briony. It is April 1940, and a large London hospital has "been emptying slowly, invisibly, for many days," (253) preparing to receive the hundreds of casualties who will be evacuated from Dunkirk. Briony, age eighteen, is a student nurse at the hospital, following in the steps of Cecilia who has become a head nurse. The sisters remain unreconciled, but it is not hard for us as readers to see in Briony's refusal to attend university and her decision to enter the nursing profession her determination to make things right with Cecilia and Robbie, to atone for her foolish adolescent lie. For although McEwan does not yet use the word "atone" to describe Briony's actions, we are tempted to do so as we recall the title of the novel. We may find ourselves looking for evidence of atonement as we read, or at least wondering how the title and story relate.

Atonement comes from the phrase "to be at one" with God. The noun *onement*, first used by John Wycliffe in the fourteenth century, presupposes an earlier estrangement, a separation so painful and so deep that it is nearly impossible to imagine how one might close the gap, bridge the chasm, reunite what has been torn apart. *Onement* thus suggests an act of atoning, a sacrifice, a deed or series of deeds that makes things right, but it also suggests a final reconciliation, the moment when two who have been at odds with each other are once again in a state of at-one-ment. When William Tyndale came to translate 2 Corinthians 5:18 in the early sixteenth century, he used the word *atonement* for the first time in an English Bible: "For God was in Christ, and made agreement between the world and himself, and imputed not their sins unto them, and hath committed to us the preaching of the atonement." Although here atonement focuses on reconciliation, on the mending of the estrangement between the world and God, later it came to have a more legal connotation. To atone for a sin meant to pay an unimaginable debt, to make right a grievous wrong. In the Christian tradition, only God himself in Christ could atone for—make sacrifice, expiation, or propitiation for—the enormous debt of sin itself.

Briony's decision to abandon her university plans and become a nurse incorporates both meanings of atonement. She desperately wants to be "at one" with Cecilia, to the point of making herself into a carbon copy of her older sister, despite the fact that she lacks a natural talent for nursing. And although she cannot pay Robbie back for the ruin of his plans or the lost years spent in prison, she can sacrifice her own dreams on the altar of altruism and spend her energies caring for soldiers who substitute for Robbie. She can repay a debt; she can make wrongs right. And she can dream about a full atonement:

> She thought too that if one of these men was Robbie, how she would dress his wounds without knowing who he was, and with cotton wool tenderly rub his face until his familiar features emerged, and how he would turn to her with gratitude, realize who she was, and take her hand, and in silently squeezing it, forgive her. Then he would let her settle him down into sleep. (281)

When we read these words, we realize that in many ways the eighteen-year-old Briony is not much different from the thirteen-year-old Briony. She still cherishes a simple plotline—sin, punishment, redemption—and she still believes and hopes that real life will imitate her art.

She is also terribly afraid that if Robbie dies in the war, she will be abandoned forever to the horror of her crime. And so the need to make reconciliation—or at least to engineer a reunion between Robbie and Cecilia—takes on its own urgency.

> Her secret torment and the public upheaval of war had always seemed separate worlds, but now she understood how the war might compound her crime. The only conceivable solution would be for the past never to have happened. If he didn't come back. . . . To Briony, it appeared that her life was going to be lived in one room, without a door. (271–72)

That one solution to her private hell might be "for the past never to have happened" seems to be the motivation for another strategy Briony employs in Part Three. Although she has abandoned her plans to go to university, she has not abandoned her ambitions to become a writer. Each night in the nurses' dormitory, she writes little vignettes of the day's events in a "foolscap notebook with marbled cardboard covers" (263), but her heart is bound up with another story she has pounded out on a borrowed typewriter in a "tempest of composition" not unlike the one that produced *The Trials of Arabella*. It is called "Two Figures by a Fountain" and of course retells the scene between Robbie and Cecilia. The story is written in a cool tone with an eye toward creating an amoral description of "pure geometry" that seeks only to reproduce "the clear light of a summer's morning, the sensations of a child standing at a window, the curve and dip of a swallow's flight over a pool of water" (265). It is a story that realizes Briony's ambition to create an "impartial psychological realism" that refuses to find a moral within the complexities of everyday life, that refuses to name actions "right" or "wrong," that resolves "wickedness and scheming" into simple "confusion and misunderstanding" (38). It is also a story that is completely false. The two figures by the fountain tussle over a Ming vase; the young woman goes into the water completely dressed; the child observes the scene; the tension dissolves; the story ends. There is no crime, no consequence, no need for atonement.

But a crime cannot be so easily erased nor atonement so cheaply purchased. So Briony undertakes a footsore, harrowing trek of her own, not across war-torn France toward Dunkirk but through the streets of London to Cecilia's flat and a strained encounter with her sister and Robbie. She tells them the truth. They all sit down together at a table, although they do not share a meal. Robbie tells Briony what to do:

> "You'll go to a solicitor, a commissioner for oaths, and make a statement which will be signed and witnessed. In it

you'll say what you did wrong, and how you're retracting your evidence. . . . Then you'll write to me in much greater detail. In this letter you'll put in absolutely everything you think is relevant. . . . It needs to be a long letter." (326)

Yes, Briony thinks, *yes*. This is what she needs to do to make things right. It is barely a reconciliation, still less an atonement—the debt is too great to be paid by a mere legal transaction—but Briony leaves the apartment soothed and comforted. Robbie and Cecilia are together, safe, and still in love. Briony has been released from the "room without a door." She is free, and she now knows "what was required of her. Not simply a letter, but a new draft, an atonement," a revision of "Two Figures by a Fountain" that will tell the whole truth (330).

Part Three concludes with a set of initials, a place, and a date: "BT, London, 1999" (330). It may take us a moment to realize that "BT" stands for Briony Tallis and that this last line is an author's signature. Then it dawns on us, perhaps with a bit of shock, that the entire book thus far has been Briony Tallis's "new draft," her atonement. The novel we have been reading is not *Atonement* by Ian McEwan; it is *Atonement* by Briony Tallis. In contrast to the cool, false narrative of "Two Figures by a Fountain," this story—the entire novel to this point—has plunged into the psychological, emotional, and moral motivations of its characters and no one has emerged unscathed. Not Emily and Jack, playing all too well their roles of patient wife, erring husband, and distant parents; not Lola and Paul in their lustful encounters and complicity with Briony's lie; certainly not Briony herself, with her romance-addled imagination and cruel moral certainty; not even Robbie and Cecilia, muddling their way through an emerging love affair. In light of this revelation of Briony's authorshhip, we become aware of new dimensions in the novel. We may now notice, for instance, that in Part Two Briony submerges her own voice to become "at one" with Robbie, recounting his journey across France as he would have experienced it, framed not just by his moment-to-moment suffering but also by the memory of Cecilia's love. Having stripped Robbie of his freedom, Briony sets out to repay her debt and restore his personhood by walking step by step with him along the war-torn boulevard. Similarly, as we look back over the slowly unfolding narrative of Part One, we may also now think of it as part of Briony's "long letter" that records, for Robbie's sake, every relevant detail.

But *Atonement*—at least Ian McEwan's *Atonement*—is not yet finished. He adds an Epilogue, titled "London, 1999," written without pretence in Briony's own voice. Here she tells us that she is seventy-seven and that she has just completed her last novel. She knows it is her last novel because the doctor has diagnosed her with vascular dementia. What lies ahead is "loss of memory, short- and long-term, the disappearance of single words . . . then language itself," surely the most frightening prognosis a writer can hear (335). Alone in her room after her birthday celebration, she muses,

> I've been thinking about my last novel, the one that should have been my first. The earliest version, January 1940, the latest, March 1999, and in between, half a dozen different drafts. . . . There was our crime—Lola's, Marshall's, mine—and from the second version onward I set out to describe it. (349)

How fortuitous, how fitting, that before her memory deserts her forever, she has been able to complete her "fifty-nine-year assignment," to revise the false 1940 "Two Figures by a Fountain" into the 1999 *Atonement*—the true version of the crime, its consequences, and yes, the atonement she has procured.

Or is it the true version? Briony continues,

I have not traveled so very far after all, since I wrote my little play. Or rather, I've made a huge digression and doubled back to my starting place. Only in this last version my lovers end well, standing side by side on a South London pavement as I walk away. All the preceding drafts were pitiless. Now I can no longer think what purpose would be served if, say, I tried to persuade my reader, by direct or indirect means, that Robbie Turner died of septicemia at Bray Dunes on 1 June 1940, or that Cecilia was killed in September of the same year by the bomb that destroyed Balham Underground Station. . . . Who would want to believe that they never met again, never fulfilled their love? Who would want to believe that, except in the service of the bleakest realism? (349–50)

Only in this last version do her lovers end well? Robbie and Cecilia both dead? It is a stunning revelation and one for which we, the readers, are entirely unprepared. Has Briony reverted in her final version to romance? Is *Atonement* just a more sophisticated version of *The Trials of Arabella*? Does the novel evade bleakest realism only to devolve into sentimentality?

Or do we need to rethink our expectations? What is a true story? Is it an account of what "really happened," or is it a narrative that speaks the truth about human beings—that they love, and suffer, and hope?

Are Briony and McEwan suggesting that if we look starkly at the world—whether that world is created by a novelist or is the one in which we actually live—we will see only a chaotic and disordered place, a cosmos where the story of a thirteen-year-old girl can send a man to jail, where a leg hangs in a tree, and where lovers are never reunited? And has the entire novel, or at least Briony's novel, been an exercise in rationalization? A relentless pursuit to cleanse her guilty conscience? Has that guilt driven her not so much to atone for her lie as to account for it?

Or is the situation even more dire? If stories are the only coherent patterns in the world, and if novelists—or God—control stories from beginning to end, if they "set the limits and the terms," then can evil ever be erased? Briony's answer is relentless: "[H]ow can a novelist achieve atonement when, with her absolute power of deciding outcomes, she is also God? There is no one, no entity or higher form that she can appeal to, or be reconciled with, or that can forgive her. . . . No atonement for God, or novelists, even if they are atheists" (350–51). Is McEwan suggesting that there is no relief from the often chaotic, unhappy stories we live? That no one can make right the grievous wrongs that spring from war, divorce, carelessness, or the almost-innocent lie of a child?

Perhaps. It may be that we cannot, in life or in novels, have the moral certitude that animates *The Trials of Arabella*. We are not promised a life—or a story—where punishment always follows sin and both are fully resolved in an act of redemption that pays the debt, rights the wrong, and reconciles the estranged. But neither are we then only left with the cool, amoral vision of "Two Figures by a Fountain" or with the "bleakest realism" that pitilessly removes love and lovers from the world. It may be that if, in this life, we do not always experience atonement, we may yet read *Atonement*. What may remain is hope—the hope of another draft, another version, "a final act of kindness, a stand against oblivion and despair" (351).

Is that enough? It is a question McEwan does not answer, but it is one that we as readers must struggle with. McEwan has said in interviews that he does not believe in God, and his references to religion, Christianity, and the church are largely ironic. Despite his criticism of the church's relevance for modern life and his argument that moral certitude is a cruel delusion, McEwan leans heavily throughout the novel on theological language. In a world split apart by betrayals and suffering and wickedness, we long for atonement. Our sense of justice and our need for hope demand it. And even as McEwan withholds it from us—there is no atonement, he says, for or from God—we sense, with him, that this is not the last word.

■ Discussion Questions about the Novel

1. The incident that sets the Tallis disaster in motion is trivial—a flirtatious disagreement between a pair of would-be lovers— but Briony's perception of the encounter has monumental consequences. To what extent are our lives the result of the stories we tell about them? What happens when the story we tell differs from the story someone else tells? Who adjudicates among competing stories?

2. Throughout Part Three, Briony says that she has committed a crime. Do you agree that her story about Robbie raping Lola was a crime? She is, after all, only a thirteen-year-old (and a rather young thirteen at that) who is trying to make sense of a frightening and confusing situation. Paul and Lola are as much, and perhaps more, to blame, as is Briony's mother, who offers so little support and moral guidance. What about Jack, the father, who does not rush home from London even when the twins are reported missing? If Briony did not commit a crime, was she still morally responsible?

3. In a novel that has many complex characters, is Paul Marshall perhaps too easily identified as a villain? Is he unfathomably stupid, as Cecilia claims? Would the novel have been better if he had been a more complicated character? Or is the notion of "simple evil" true to our experience of wickedness in this world?

4. Is it possible ever to forget ourselves entirely and unselfishly think only of someone else? Is it possible not to be the hero of the stories we tell about ourselves and others? For instance, even while Briony is trying to made amends with Robbie and Cecilia, she cannot help but take "calm pleasure" in announcing the wedding of Paul Marshall and Lola Quincey and seeing her sister's reaction to the news (327).

5. A number of Christian thinkers and theologians have used the analogy of the novelist's relationship with his or her characters to describe the relationship between God and humankind as one of inscribed freedom—the freedom of the characters (or people) to move under the authorial pen of the novelist (or God). Does McEwan seem to be drawing on this picture or on some other version of the novelist/God comparison? What does it mean for Briony to say, "There is no atonement for God, or novelists?"

6. Those of us who like to read often think of life as a story, but more often than not we imagine that our stories will have happy endings. McEwan adds an edge of terror, and responsibility, to the notion of life as story. Does that make you more or less likely to continue to use the metaphor?

7. *Atonement* is a word that seems almost exclusively to belong to our religious experiences. A near-synonym, *redemption*, is used much more broadly. We redeem time and reputations and even coupons. But atonement stands starkly within our religious vocabulary. How does the title *Atonement* guide your reading of the novel? Would the novel lose any of its power if it were titled *Redemption* or *Reconciliation* or *Renewal*?

◼ Other Books to Consider

—Tony Earley, *Jim the Boy*. Boston: Little, Brown, 2000.

> In the 1930s, young Jim begins to grow up—and though his childhood has been in the secure and safe company of his loving mother and uncles, he will now begin to understand and confront the family secrets that destroyed all unity in the previous generation.

—Clyde Edgerton, *The Floatplane Notebooks*. Chapel Hill, NC: Algonquin Books, 1988.

> The Copeland family of Listre, North Carolina, gathers every May to clean up the family graveyard and to recall the generational stories that have bound them together as a family. These are stories that suggest anguish and grace, pain and reconciliation, and by the end of the novel, the heartsick are healed—though in ways no family would ever expect—or perhaps forgive.

—James McBride, *Miracle at St. Anna*. New York: Riverhead Books, 2002.

> Inspired by a historical incident at St. Anna in Tuscany, this is a story of four American soldiers who take refuge from the war and who are supported by the partisans—and of the miracle that they all encounter because of a young Italian boy.

—Alice McDermott, *After This*. New York: Farrar, Straus and Giroux, 2006.

> Set during the Vietnam era, this is the story of one American family whose parents and four children find their traditional Catholic world grating against the cultural freedoms as well as the looming presence of war that marked the 1960s. In that grating, they work, sometimes together, sometimes not, to understand the new meaning and power of family.

Integrative Discussion Questions
for Part Three

1. *Peace like a River*, *Life of Pi*, and *Atonement* all trace a child's passage into adulthood. Are there any differences in these portrayals? Why does this transition pass in each case through violence and death? Which novel would work best with a teenage audience? Are these "young adult novels," or do they require the experience of adulthood?

2. All three novels in this section emphasize the presence of the storyteller and all of them undercut the notion that the storyteller is to be trusted without question. In fact, alternate readings are suggested to the reader, readings which cannot both be true. What do authors gain by highlighting the presence of the author? What do authors gain by crafting a narrative that leaves the reader with ambiguity? In presenting spiritual questions, is ambiguity an ethical choice for an author?

3. Reuben Land, Pi Patel, and Briony, the storytellers in these three novels, have specific goals in their telling. Are their goals similar? For example, does Pi seek atonement? Does Briony seek to bear witness? Does Reuben seek understanding? To what degree are Reuben, Pi, and Briony in control of their stories? Do all narrators have specific goals as storytellers? In what ways might an understanding of those goals cloud or clarify a novel's spiritual meanings?

PART FOUR

"It Is Well with My Soul"

"It Is Well
with My Soul"

In a 1964 letter describing his understanding of Dante's *The Divine Comedy*, Karol Woytyła, who would become Pope John Paul II fourteen years later, wrote that the poem was "the history of [Dante's] creative search and, above all, the history of his love." It is an unusual description, the journey through hell and purgatory as the history of the writer's creative search, and the history of his love. Must the search for creativity and for love move through hell itself before it can ascend to the mountains of heaven?

Must the barrenness and grief of hell precede the affirmations and joys of heaven?

The characters of Frederick Buechner's *Godric*, Oscar Hijuelos's *Mr. Ives' Christmas*, and Olga Grushin's *The Dream Life of Sukhanov* know these questions. Each experiences a time of terrible suffering and loss. Mr. Ives, for example, loses his son in a senseless and random murder, a fact of which he is reminded each Christmas. This grief could easily destroy him; certainly it seems to deal a deathblow to any vitality in his faith. But the time comes when, almost secretly, that vitality begins to green again. There is a time to mourn, and a time to dance, and though for Ives those two times are not distinct and separate, the fact that he does move toward forgiveness and faith leads us, in the end, to a novel filled with hope.

The journey on the Emmaus road is a journey from despair to a surprising hopefulness and an ecstatic joy. Eyes open, and old words are heard with new ears. It is a principle understood by Horatio G. Spafford, who wrote the words to "It Is Well with My Soul" after the loss of several of his children. Godric, Mr. Ives, and Sukhanov understand that principle as well.

GODRIC   Frederick Buechner
(1980)

Synopsis

Godric of Finchale ("finkle"), an English saint, lives a life of solitude and penance by the River Wear. An innocent, idealistic monk named Reginald has been sent to record Godric's life for posterity, and the novel unfolds as a series of haphazard flashbacks in which Godric recalls the major events of his long life. Godric vehemently resists the holy whitewashing Reginald would give the narrative, however, and persistently emphasizes the grit and grime of his story.

Born in the middle of the eleventh century to a family of starving peasants, Godric's only comfort in his childhood seems to have been his deep friendship—bordering at times on romance—with his sister Burcwen. The adolescent Godric leaves home as soon as possible. After brief successes in selling fake relics, Godric falls into company with Roger Mouse, with whom he buys a ship and amasses a small fortune as a pirate. Throughout his pirate days, Godric repeatedly returns to the Isle of Farne to hide his treasure and also to converse with the spirit of St. Cuthbert, who appears to him there and offers spiritual guidance.

On a pilgrimage to Rome, Godric meets Gillian, a beautiful and mysterious woman who appears only to Godric and who, like St. Cuthbert, encourages Godric to reform his life. But upon returning from Rome, Godric becomes a steward for the local nobleman Falkes de Granvill, enforcing ruthless taxation of the poor. Through a series of events, Godric next finds himself in the Holy

Land. He undergoes a true conversion in the Jordan River and walks his way back to England on bare feet.

In his home country, Godric takes the hidden treasure from Farne and leaves it on the altar of a church tended by Elric, a holy madman who shows him the ropes of the ascetic life. Godric soon settles into his own homely hermitage on the River Wear, where he is befriended by two snakes named Tune and Fairweather. In time, he is also joined by his mother Aedwen, his brother William, and his sister Burcwen, but the family is rent apart by betrayals and tragedy. The story ends with Godric's death, but the novel ends with an unctuous postscript by Reginald, which retells Godric's life in the terms that the old man has been railing against for the entire novel.

On the Author

Frederick Buechner's (b. 1926) first novel, *A Long Day's Dying*, received glowing reviews when it was published in 1950. Buechner disappointed his critics slightly with his next two novels, and he positively baffled them with *The Final Beast* in 1965. What confused the critics was not only the fact that Buechner, a thoughtful agnostic, had chosen to write a novel about a struggling minister, but also that by the time of the publication of *The Final Beast* he had chosen to become a minister himself. He enrolled in Union Theological Seminary in 1954, becoming ordained in 1958. Thereafter, most of Buechner's fiction involved religious themes and characters. Before *Godric*, Buechner's major literary work was *The Book of Bebb* (1971–77), a collection of four novels centering around enigmatic Leo Bebb, a nutty Southern salesman-turned-preacher who is either a charlatan or a saint—or both.

In addition to writing fiction, Buechner has published sermon collections, theological reflections, and several memoirs. The memoirs are masterfully written, and they reveal a rich and moving life story, including the suicide of his father when Buechner was a young boy, Buechner's own religious struggles as a young man, his seminary enrollment that seems to have surprised him as much as anyone, and the mature reflections of a caring father. The memoir *Now and Then* covers the time in Buechner's life when he wrote *Godric*.

Godric was published in 1980 and nominated for the Pulitzer Prize in 1981. In *Now and Then* Buechner judged his own work, fairly accurately, as too secular for religious readers and too religious for secular readers. Since that time, his writing seems to have tipped this balance in the latter direction. He has continued to produce moving memoirs and spiritual nonfiction, and his few novels have tended to retell the stories of saints and biblical heroes. *The Son of Laughter* (1993), probably the closest of these books to *Godric* in substance and style, tells the story of Jacob (brother of Esau); *Brendan* (1987) recounts the life of the Irish St. Brendan; *On the Road With the Archangel* (1997) is a brief but lively version of the apocryphal *Book of Tobit*.

Considering the Novel

Readers who finish *Godric* usually describe the book as a saint's life, and they tend to recall how the story swirls together themes of sinfulness and saintliness. The book begins, however, not with the complexities of sainthood but the realities of simple friendship. Before *Godric* is ever a story about the struggle of holiness against sin, it is a more mundane story about common friendship and the pain that inadvertently but inevitably comes with it. Perhaps "common friendship" is the wrong term—two of Godric's five friends are real snakes, after all—but the kinds of relationships that Godric enjoys and endures with his friends should be readily familiar to any human reader. They are very realistic relationships, partly because Godric insists that friendship always entails suffering. "That's five friends," he says near the end of his first entry, "one for each of Jesu's wounds, and Godric bears their marks still on what's left of him as in their time they all bore his on them. What's friendship, when all's done, but the giving and taking of wounds?" (7).

The novel is filled with examples of loved ones wounding one another, frequently through abandonment. Godric sends away his beloved serpents already in the first paragraph, and throughout the story he himself repeatedly abandons his friends—especially Burcwen, but also the rest of his family and the lady Hedwic, a young woman brutalized by her much older husband. In his own mind, Godric abandons these people not despite his love for them but *because* of that love. "The worst that Godric ever did," he explains, "he did for love. Nor was it of an earthy sort that seeks its own but love that gives itself away for the beloved's sake, and thus, when all is said and done, the love that God himself commands" (155). Doing the worst for love is a habit bred in Godric's bones. His own father, Aedlward, has made a lifestyle out of lovingly deserting his family in order to feed them. It is not only family members who abandon one another. Godric and Mouse part violently, and even the gentle Gillian vanishes completely from Godric's life, "[taking] with her all but the husk of Godric's joy" (7).

Although Godric himself describes such pain as the natural—if unintended—consequence of human love, the various situations presented throughout the book offer an even more complicated reflection on the subject. Love does not always cause suffering; sometimes love is simply overcome by other circumstances. Which is more responsible for Aedlward's neglect of his family, for instance: his love for them or their desperate poverty? Would it have been better for him to stay at home, so that the five of them could starve together as a happy family? Godric himself might suggest that it is love itself that inflicts wounds, but the novel offers situations where love is simply overwhelmed by circumstances beyond the characters' control. Godric explains his distance from Hedwic in terms that make him seem guilty: "So for love of her I wounded her by keeping from her sight, and thus my love stung both of us like hate" (86). A reader might well wonder, however, whether love itself can truly sting like hate. A more accurate assessment of the situation might be the one Godric himself provides earlier on the same page: "What a net of sin I'd gotten tangled in."

Godric does offer a more positive picture of friendship later in the novel, where he describes it as two people reaching out to one another from different rocks in Wear: "The water races in between with strength enough to kill. But each of us reached out to touch the other, and our friendship was the comfort of that touch" (96). These words seem to answer Godric's early question of what friendship is beyond the giving and taking of wounds. Throughout most of the novel, however, friendship is more of a crushing burden than a comforting touch. It is not a stone to stand on, but a load to lift. "'Your father lies beneath a stone,' old Aedwen mumbles, dozing at her wheel, and Godric thinks how it's a stone they're all beneath. The stone is need and hurt and gall and tongue-tied longing, for that's the stone that kinship always bears, yet the loss of it would press more grievous still" (54). Home is where the hurt is.

Godric literally bears this hurtful stone throughout the novel: he is forever carrying the ones he loves. He lifts Burcwen out of the tree where she has waited for him to leave home, and he lifts her back into the tree before he goes. He carries his mother when she twists her ankle on their trip to Rome. He carries Elric through the snow. Late in the novel, it is finally Godric's own turn to be carried when Perkin bears him to Wear for the last time.

The strain and pain of human love is a moving theme in *Godric*, not only because it offers recognizable human relationships, but because it enables readers to connect more intimately to a greater paradox: the perpetual struggle between saintliness and sin. Godric's family relationships in some ways mirror his spiritual ones. It is for love of his earthly father's soul that Godric suffers the trip to Rome; it is for love of God that he walks without shoes, pinches his flesh between sheets of iron, and freezes his bones in Wear. If his loved ones become literal burdens for Godric throughout the novel, so too does Christ, whose first miraculous revelation comes upon Godric as the dead weight of an enormous fish, "a hundredweight of fillet which he laid across his shoulders so that like a bishop's stole it hung down low to either side." It is not an easy mantle to bear:

His burden dragged him under, yet he would not let it go, for though the deep churned dark about him, still deeper in his heart he saw that porpoise eye so blithe in death and heard its voice, or so he thought, say, "Take and eat me, Godric, to thy soul's delight. Hold fast to him who gave his life for thee and thine." Godric's breath then failed him. He was sucked down by the tide. (15)

This Jesus fish is no silver magnet for affixing to the back of one's car; it is a crushing load. Christ himself becomes a burden for Godric, and his loving but burdensome human relationships thus serve as analogs for his relationship to Christ. From the very first chapter, the suffering of human friendship serves as a meditation on the suffering of Christ: five friends, one for each of Jesu's wounds.

It is well that Buechner approaches issues of spiritual suffering through believable human relationships, because few modern readers can readily identify with Godric's sharp asceticism. Over two millenia, the Christian tradition has included a vast array of ascetic practices, ranging from gentle forms of self-denial, such as fasting and celibacy, to more severe forms of self-punishment, such as flagellation. Buechner does not flinch from the violence of Godric's austere spirituality, although some readers may flinch as they read about it. For readers unaccustomed to ascetic traditions, the practices of medieval hermits might seem troubling both emotionally and theologically. Buechner does seem aware of this. He places the strongest statements of ascetic theology in the hyperbolic mouth of Elric: "For every hour that I sting with pain, Christ stings an hour less" (109–10). Godric's own explanations of asceticism are less precise. He goes unshod to honor Jesus, who "walked barefoot up to Calvary" (106); the nip of Godric's iron vest, he says, is "to chasten me and keep me mindful of the crueler nips our Savior bore" (81). His ascetic sufferings ultimately amount to little more than disciplined meditation—an acceptable and even admirable practice in the minds of most twenty-first century Christians. Godric punishes himself not to reduce Christ's torments but merely to understand them more fully.

Nevertheless, Godric remains an extravagant character in all respects—both secular and spiritual—and the descriptions of his self-punishments might unsettle some readers:

Time and again, with rage, I hurl my back against the stone to punish stone and back as well until my irons clank like hammers on a forge. My beard is stuck with straws from

sleeping. My eyes are wild. I clank my flesh so raw I roar with
pain. Poor Reginald's aghast and blocks his ears. (81)

It is easy—just this once—to side with Reginald. Although the
scene certainly illustrates the sheer fervor of Godric's devotion to
Christ, some Christian readers might question whether torturing
oneself is a fitting form of devotion. Such passages will be deeply
moving to some readers, potentially alienating to others—and
perhaps darkly fascinating for a third group. Perhaps that is why
Buechner does not rely heavily on such scenes to articulate the
deep themes of love and suffering. That's what friends and family
are for.

Buechner's primary purpose in *Godric*, of course, is not to
preach asceticism among modern audiences, but to complicate
the stereotype of a saint. He does this by manipulating both
his plot and his characters. The plot, for example, repeatedly
violates chronological order—a sharp departure from typical
biographies of saints. Medieval hagiographies (or saints'
lives, sometimes simply called *vitas*) typically offer very linear
narratives in order to demonstrate a sure and steady process of
spiritual maturity. The protagonist's childhood is scrutinized for
signs of nascent saintliness. Any sins in the person's early life
serve only to contrast with the purity and holiness of the hero
who eventually emerges.

Godric, however, confounds such linear chronology by talking
in circles. "I've told my life from both its ends at once," he
confesses—and he might have added: "and also from every point
in between." He recalls, for instance, a time when he and Ailred
escaped the flooded river by climbing onto the roof of his little
chapel. From within this flashback, he launches into yet another
flashback: he tells Ailred of his trip to Rome. "And as I told him
how we went," Godric says, "what used to be became what was,

as now again it does become what is" (59). The verbs in the very next sentence shift from the past to the present tense ("It *is* the Lady month of May, and all *is* green"), a curious choice for someone who has just made two leaps *backward* in time. Such shifts are common throughout the novel, and they help Godric in his struggle against any linear interpretation of his life. Because time itself seems to have little meaning for Godric, the sins of his younger days continually clutter his heart and soul.

It is entirely appropriate for Buechner to thus clutter the structure of the book by repeating important ideas, because doing so makes Godric more human both intellectually and morally. Intellectually, Godric's mind is as disordered as most human minds; the book shows us a perfectly average stream of consciousness. Morally, Godric is both a sinner and a saint. The sins of his younger days still linger in his crowded mind. The haphazard arrangement of events does not suggest carelessness on Buechner's part, therefore, but rather his deliberate development of Godric's character.

Manipulation of character is the second way in which Buechner complicates the stereotype of a saint. The characters of Reginald and Godric allow him to poke fun at the ways in which medieval writing idealized the lives of saints. Biographies of saints typically portrayed holy men and women as scarcely human heroes, destined by God to work wonders, slay demons, and confound the forces of evil. This kind of writing is primarily represented by Reginald, who is arguably the most ridiculous character in the book (despite serious competition from Peregrine Small). Reginald is useful, however, insofar as he allows Buechner to dismiss hagiographic elements that might seem laughable to modern audiences while nevertheless including them in the book. Skeptics who would snicker at an actual medieval saint's life will find Godric—and Buechner—snickering right along with them during Reginald's speeches.

The most obvious complication Buechner introduces to the hagiographic tradition is, of course, the character of Godric himself. Buechner cleverly gives Godric a voice in his own biography. Most saints' lives are told in the third person. In fact, a third-person narrator would seem to be a necessary feature of a saint's life, because one common characteristic of saints is that they rarely think of themselves as saints. "Since holiness was all he knew," Godric says of St. Cuthbert, "I think he did not know his own" (38). Godric himself roars at the title of "saint," insisting that he is a wretched sinner.

Does Buechner want us to believe him? When we consider Godric's visions and his healing touch, it seems undeniable that there is something saintly about the man, something more than stink and rage. There is much to love in Godric: his earnest intensity, his honest struggle, his rough humility. There is also, however, much about Godric to dislike—even the old Godric, who has allegedly acknowledged the errors of his youth. His manner with Reginald, for example, at times borders on cruelty. It is easy to understand why someone would want to ignore Reginald, but Godric seems delighted to harass him just for the sport of it. More seriously, Godric yields to incest with his sister after he has already spent several years repenting of—among other things—sins of the flesh.

Perhaps the most off-putting aspect of Godric's character is the way in which he remembers his earlier pirate days. He describes how Roger Mouse was so busy raping pilgrims on the *Saint Esprit* that he forgot to rob them. "I broke my bonds," old Godric recalls, "and doused him with a pail of chill, grey sea. But Mouse was plunged so deep into his work, I think he never even knew" (48). The passage is so playful, almost whimsical with its double entendre, that a reader is tempted to overlook the sheer ugliness of what is actually happening to the woman being raped. It is not merely the young sinner "Deric" who dismisses Mouse's wickedness, but old Godric himself. Young Deric at least attempts to interrupt the scene with a pail of cold water, but Godric, reliving the episode with the benefit of hindsight, seems eager to look past the horror of rape. "Nonetheless," he immediately continues, "our fights were few those first, far days. We loved each other, Mouse and I . . ." (48).

In fact, Godric explicitly dismisses Mouse's behavior in the first chapter, where he acknowledges that Mouse was a sinner, but insists that "there was less room left in him for truly mortal sin than in your landlocked, penny-pinching chapmen. . . . Mouse's sin smacked less of evil than of larkishness, the likes of which Our Lord himself could hardly help but wink at when he spied it out in whore and prodigal. I loved Mouse" (4). Isn't this old saint—who seems so painfully sensitive to his own sinfulness and the suffering of others—callously dismissive of a truly cruel act? Passages such as this flashback make it easy to take Godric at his word when he insists that he is a corrupt sinner even in his old age.

It would have been easy for Buechner to write a modernized version of Godric's life by giving the holy old man a few gruff and gritty quirks to prove that the saint is human. What Buechner has done, however, is something more complex and daring. He has developed the flesh-and-blood sins of his protagonist to the point where they could easily overwhelm that character's saintly virtues. Just as Godric seems suspended between heavenly visions and hellish lusts, so his character hangs between an appealing saintliness and an appalling sinfulness in the mind of a reader.

One last feature of *Godric* deserves mention, and it is frequently the first thing readers notice: the very odd style. "I've never learned to wrap my tongue round courtly talk. The only words I know are words of wood and stone fit best for rough, unlettered folk like me" (100). Many readers are surprised to learn that Godric's style—like the structure of his story—is utterly unanchored in time. It is certainly not typical of literature written in the early twelfth century, when the historical Godric lived and breathed. Buechner seems to have given Godric not the speech patterns of real Saxons, but literary flourishes of later authors whom Buechner admires. In terms of rhythm, Godric's speech is closer to the iambic pentameter of Shakespeare and Milton (sixteenth and seventeenth centuries); in terms of word choice, it is closer to the vibrant earthiness of Gerard Manley Hopkins (nineteenth century). Buechner's goal is obviously not historical accuracy but a kind of distancing effect, because this is one of the best ways to reinvigorate old ideas. It allows readers to experience familiar truths almost as if these truths were new.

The style of *Godric* is masterful in many ways, but it does not always serve one basic function of style in a novel, which is to clearly distinguish characters from one another. The one character in the book with a truly distinct style, of course, is Reginald. The rough profundity of Godric's own speech is employed indiscriminately in the mouths of several characters. Consider, for example, the following quotations:

The waves are like the years the way they melt. (44)
Time is a storm. Times past and times to come, they heave and flow and leap their bounds like Wear. (60)

These lines sound so much like Godric himself that even an attentive reader could understandably mistake their speakers (Roger Mouse and Ailred, respectively).

Nevertheless, the style of *Godric* may be its most successful literary feature. While it is true that the most meaningful lines lose little or nothing if taken out of context, most readers will nevertheless find those lines moving. "What's lost is nothing to what's found, and all the death that ever was, set next to life, would scarcely fill a cup" (96). Even if one does not remember where this sentence appears in the novel or how it contributes to the story, it remains a stirring line, profound, exuberant, and joyful.

■ Discussion Questions about the Novel

1. How do you respond to Godric's confession that "the worst [he] ever did, he did for love" (155)? In saying this, is he expressing regret for unintended consequences, or is he simply rationalizing some of the hurtful choices he has made? Consider, for example, his abandonment of Burcwen when he leaves home, or his abandonment of the lady Hedwic. Does Godric's love actually cause these people to suffer, or is his love for them superseded by other motives?

2. Bird imagery fills the book. Godric's own nose is described as a beak. The holy Isle of Farne is covered with birds. In the grim squalor of Rome, Godric notices a trapped bird beating his wings above the altar (65). What do such images suggest about Godric and his story?

3. What is the character of Elric doing in this story? On the one hand, he seems to be a more extreme version of Godric himself. Perhaps he is a sort of lightning rod for skepticism: readers who dislike ascetic practices will channel their frustration toward Elric (just as those who would dislike a traditional hagiography are warmly invited to sneer at Reginald). Godric's asceticism is mild in contrast to Elric's. On the other hand, does Elric's lifestyle merely advertise in large capital letters

the very ideas and beliefs that are writ small in Godric's own story—but written there nonetheless? How does the character of Elric affect your attitude toward Godric?

4. When Godric identifies Cuthbert as a saint, Cuthbert deflects the label. "Ah well," he says. "To Gossip Guillemot I'm just a bald head like an egg. To God, who knows?" (38). When Reginald refers to Godric as a saint at the end of his life, Godric positively roars. Are there important differences between Cuthbert and Godric, or by the end of the novel does Godric seem to have reached the point where Cuthbert was in the beginning? Does it seem to you that Cuthbert, if allowed to tell his own tale, would tell a story as rough and ready as Godric's?

5. It is easy to snicker at Reginald's sanctimonious revision of Godric's life when we have Godric's own version surrounding it. But how might we valorize heroes from our own past or present? How would our versions of their stories differ from the stories these heroes might tell about themselves?

6. In his book *Wishful Thinking: A Theological ABC* (1973), Buechner advises anyone with even a little knowledge of a foreign language to read the Bible in that language, because the Bible can become too familiar when repeatedly experienced in one's own tongue. In *Godric*, Buechner attempts to create this effect by making the English language itself sound foreign and fresh. Are there any lines that you found particularly invigorating?

7. In his autobiography *Now and Then* (1983), Buechner explains that, at the time he was writing *Godric*, his daughters had just

moved away to school, leaving their father to write his books and muse on the fact that his own deep love for them was now causing him pain. Does the novel capture any of your own feelings when you first moved away from home, or sent children away to school, or experienced some other parting from those you love?

▨ Other Books to Consider

—Frederick Buechner, *Brendan*. New York: Harper Collins, 1987.

> In the novel that followed *Godric*, Buechner chronicles the life of the sixth-century Irish saint, following his lifelong search for the earthly paradise.

—Pierre de Calan, *Cosmas, or the Love of God*. Garden City, NY: Doubleday, 1980.

> When Cosmas comes to the Abbey of La Trappe to fulfill his vocation as a Cistercian monk, he is eager and passionate. But his eagerness and passion are unable to get past the small details of mundane life that must be lived, even inside a monastery. His struggle with the mixture of the human and holy informs the conflict of the book, a struggle that ends with tragedy.

—Hermann Hesse, *Siddhartha*. New York: New Directions Publishing, 1951.

> When Siddhartha, a young Indian pilgrim, meets the Buddha, he is at first inclined toward discipleship. But this is not the path he takes; his own path toward a spiritual life runs through doubt, sensuality, guilt, and temptation—until he finally emerges to a true renunciation and sense of self.

—Garret Keizer, *A Dresser of Sycamore Trees*. New York: Viking, 1991.

> This nonfiction memoir chronicles Keizer's own movement into the Episcopal ministry, where he will eventually serve the community of Island Pond in Vermont's Northeast Kingdom. Carefully attuned to his own strengths and foibles and those of his parishioners, Keizer points always to a fascination with the workings of God in small and powerful ways.

—Elie Wiesel, *Souls on Fire: Portraits and Legends of Hasidic Masters*. New York: Random House, 1972.

> An engrossing collection of tales of the eighteenth- and nineteenth-century masters who founded and established the Hasidic movement, Wiesel's tales are meant to suggest how powerfully God's presence can infuse the immediate world and how legends can speak to the anguish of modern humanity.

MR. IVES' CHRISTMAS Oscar Hijuelos
(1995)

Synopsis

This novel might well have been entitled *Mr. Ives'*
Christmases. As a child, the main character, Edward Ives, is
abandoned at a foundling home during Christmas time, and a
few years later he is adopted at Christmas by a kind man who
passes on his deep, sincere Catholic faith to his son. During
another Christmas season, Ives has a near-death experience,
followed by a mystical vision as he walks down Madison
Avenue in New York City. This vision haunts Ives throughout
the rest of his life. Ives maintains his faith as he marries and
has two children, a son and a daughter. His son, Robert, feels
called to the priesthood, but during yet another Christmas
time, shortly before entering seminary, a teenager arbitrarily
murders him. Ives struggles to live on after such sorrow. He
begins to doubt God's goodness, even his existence, as he falls
into despair. He also struggles to forgive the shooter who is
released from prison less than four years after the crime. Ives
carries his grievous wound into old age. He remains a good
and kind man, but as his faith crumbles, he "gradually turned
into stone: a civil, good-hearted man, but one made of stone
all the same" (9–10). Yet by continuing to be faithful to his
wife and to the Church, even though he has lost all feelings
of devotion, Ives remains open to God's healing grace. A
breakthrough occurs after he embraces and forgives his son's
killer. At the end of his life, his love for his wife and his God
are restored, and Ives is healed as he experiences once again
the vision he has longed for since the death of his son.

On the Author

The child of parents who emigrated from Cuba in the 1940s, Oscar Hijuelos (b. 1951) was born and raised in a bilingual home in a multicultural, working class neighborhood in West Harlem, New York. Hijuelos grew up immersed in Cuban Catholic culture, which, in his words, combined the "superstition and spiritualism of Afro-Cuban religion" with Catholic Christianity. He attended public schools and received BA and MA degrees in English at City University of New York. After college, Hijuelos worked for a print advertising agency located on Madison and 41st street. He managed the company's advertising in the subway and synchronized the subway clocks, experiences he draws upon in his characterization of Mr. Ives. He published his first novel, *Our House in the Last World*, in 1983, winning the Rome Prize in 1985.

Hijuelos became the first Hispanic American winner of the Pulitzer Prize in fiction for his novel *The Mambo Kings Play Songs of Love* (1990), made into a major motion picture in 1992 under the title *The Mambo Kings*. He followed this novel with *The Fourteen Sisters of Emilio Montez O'Brien* (1993) and *Mr. Ives' Christmas* (1995); the latter novel has steadily risen in popularity, largely through book clubs and by word of mouth. More recently, Hijuelos has published *Empress of the Splendid Season* (1999), which continues his focus upon the lives of Cuban Americans in New York, and *A Simple Habana Melody* (2002), in which Hijuelos depicts life in Cuba before the mass emigration to the United States.

Considering the Novel

Mr. Ives' Christmas describes the struggle to maintain faith in a fallen world. In the opening section of the novel, "Long Ago at Christmas," we are introduced to Edward Ives (referred to simply as Ives throughout the book), a young artist working for a Madison Avenue advertising agency in the 1950s. The title of the section, "Long Ago . . . ," and the first words of the novel, "Years ago . . . ," invoke a sense of nostalgia. Early on, we are told that Ives' son Robert was shot randomly a few days before Christmas in 1967, just before his entrance into seminary to study for the priesthood. This event breaks Ives' life in two, and most of the novel is about his attempts to overcome the debilitating effects of this horrible event.

But before we learn of this deep psychic wound, we first look back at Ives in church during Christmas time, before the death of his son. In a beautifully written scene, Hijuelos evokes the splendor of the church and the power of Ives' longing evoked by such beauty. At the Festival of Faith and Writing at Calvin College, Hijuelos noted how strongly his work as an artist has been influenced by his Catholic upbringing, especially his memory of churches and the Mass: "I have never been able to resist writing about my Catholicism. All the incense, the rituals fascinated me. I can't avoid references back to my childhood. My Catholicism exists in my books as surely as the sun or sky." But Ives is not only fascinated by the beauty of the Church's art and ritual. He is moved most of all by the true meaning of the holiday for Christians: the remembrance of the birth of Jesus. It is fitting that the novel opens with this scene in the church, for it is this faith that Ives must cling to if he is to survive after his son's murder.

Even as he contemplates the birth of the Savior of the world, Ives feels the tug of grief and despair, as the image of Christ's birth in a stable reminds him of his own beginning in an orphanage. He contrasts Jesus, "the most wanted child in the history of the world," with his own origins as "an unwanted child" (4). As we witness his powerful emotional reaction, we may wonder how much of his faith is based upon the imaginative, illusory desire of an orphan for a father to provide him with safety and protection from a harsh world. Consider, for example, how Ives describes his feelings when speaking with the priests after the Mass: "He'd almost feel like a child again in their presence, safe and secure and welcome" (46). The description of Ives' prayer in church as a "wish" during a "slightly hypnotic state" (51) suggests that his faith may be largely or even entirely a fantasy of wish fulfillment (as Freud argued). After the murder of his son, Ives himself struggles to evaluate the authenticity of his faith in God.

Being abandoned by his parents has shaped Ives' identity. Because his origins are unknown, his darker complexion and hair cause him to be identified by others as Italian, Jewish, or Hispanic, highlighting in part the fictional nature of "racial" identity. Without a clear sense of ethnic identity, Ives clings to his faith to define himself. As Hijuelos describes him in an interview, Mr. Ives "makes Catholicism the strongest aspect of his identity. Without any certainty of his true identity, he is a perpetual outsider. He takes on the mantle of faith like a nationality." Ives does develop an affinity for Cuban culture, even learning to speak Spanish, and he chooses to raise his family in a multiethnic neighborhood in the inner city, rather than moving to the suburbs or country. But later, these choices make him feel guilty for putting his son in harm's way.

In addition to blaming himself, Ives also has moments in which he blames God; though he struggles valiantly against these feelings, "Ives still had days when he blamed his son's death on God's will" (8). Ives struggles to understand how an omnipotent God could allow evil and suffering to continue. He questions God's justice, and his anger at God is reinforced as the newspaper headlines repeat a common clichéd response to the death of a loved one: "GOD HAS CALLED HIM TO HEAVEN," as if God himself planned Robert's murder.

Not surprisingly, the murder of his son causes Ives to question God's existence: at times "he would think of just how much his son had loved his life and had loved God, and Ives would doubt that God existed" (10). Yet Ives continues to at least *desire* to believe in God, hoping that a revelation will come to him from outside to assure him of his son's place in heaven. Especially around Christmas,

> Ives would plaintively wait for a sign that his son, who'd deserved so much more than what he had been given, was somewhere safe and beloved by God. Each day he awaited a slick of light to enter the darkness. And when life went on as usual, without any revelation, he'd await his own death and the new life or—as he often suspected—the new oblivion to begin. (10)

Ives' faith, like Job's, is tested. His struggle to reaffirm his faith despite his doubts is summarized toward the end of the novel: "It meant despairing about the supernatural and yet waiting every night for a supernatural event" (142). Despite his despair, Ives continues to wait for God to come and explain himself.

Ives has good reason to hope for a supernatural revelation, because he himself had received a mystical vision years before the death of his son. As a result of this vision, Ives believes that "he once had a small, if imperfect, spiritual gift" (4), a gift he lovingly passes on to his son, who seems, like Ives, to have a "talent" for religion. Ives' mystical experience occurs after a near-death experience in a falling elevator. But while plunging to what he thinks is his death, Ives only feels fear, not faith, and his only desire is to grab the breasts of Miss Feingold, the woman in the elevator with him. While this can be taken as a sign of sexual desire, it can also be read as a kind of regression to infancy, a subconscious expression of his desire for a mother's safety and comfort, a desire for the mother he never knew. As he contemplates his impending death, Ives recalls an experience in childhood in which he nearly drowned. In both near-death experiences, Ives feels only fear; he doubts the existence of an afterlife. Consequently, he suspects that his faith is false, that it is "nothing more than a construct" (98). The psychological origins of his despair are revealed as the narrator describes "a sense of worthlessness coming over his foundling soul" (99). Ives feels like an "unwanted child," unworthy of being rescued or saved.

Nevertheless, he is saved from his fall, and afterward the building clock appears "oddly aglow with a kind of benevolent, supernatural light," and the people who rescue him, as well as bystanders, now appear "to be radiating what Ives could only define as goodness, as if they were angels, sent to reassure him during a crucial moment of doubt" (99). As Ives leaves the building, he has a powerful mystical vision. First he has the sensation that his eyesight suddenly improves radically, reminiscent of the common metaphor for conversion: "I was blind but now I see." Ives then experiences a "moment of pure clarity" (100) that makes him feel euphoric, as he senses all the goodness of the world swirling around him, as if the physical world had broken loose from the laws of physics. And finally, Ives has a vision of four rushing winds swirling through the sky from every direction.

Ives' first response to the vision is to feel a "thorough love for all things" (102). He is suddenly struck by the miraculous nature of his own body. As he looks at his reflection, his face looks like the face of saint, and then in the next moment, like the face of St. Paul after being struck by lightning in his blinding vision on the road to Damascus. Like many of the prophets and saints in the

Christian tradition, Ives feels both fear and awe when faced with God's revelation.

After this vision, Ives meets an old woman who notices his joy and asks if he is always so cheerful during Christmas time. Ives responds that he just had a "vision of God's presence in the world" (102). The woman looks at him as if he were crazy, and from that point on, Ives begins to question the meaning and purpose of the vision. First, he wonders why the vision happened to him, asking the first question often raised by those who suffer: "Why me?" Then he wonders why the vision did not seem to be specifically Christian. Later this will cause him to look for answers in pagan spiritualism and New Age versions of spirituality, represented especially by the figure of A. I. Explixa, a guru whom Ives hopes can explicate the meaning of his vision. He begins to read books on "science fiction or fantasy or religion," implying that religion might be just another kind of fiction or fantasy.

Ives next doubts the authenticity of the vision, explaining it away as a psychological response to his near-death experience. But the power and persistence of his memory of the vision causes him to reject this natural explanation. He is convinced that he saw something supernatural, but he can't interpret its significance. During sleepless nights, as he ponders the meaning of the vision, Ives recalls his childhood image of heaven as a "perpetual childhood" in a return to the Garden of Eden. (Freud would take this as support for his contention that religious belief is "infantile.") Now this sentimental view of heaven is replaced by a darker, more troubling view: "Ives came to believe that what he had seen—or imagined—was a picture of a bleak, otherworldly future" (105).

So what begins as an experience of the goodness of God, the goodness of his creation, and of the impending glory of life in heaven, ends up being interpreted by Ives as a revelation of a chaotic universe in which belief in a heavenly afterlife is replaced by a sense that death leads only to oblivion. What he first receives as a sign sent to reassure him of his faith and belief in God ends up leading Ives into doubt, confusion, and fear, and he shares the vision with no one.

After the random, senseless murder of Robert, Ives' is plunged into further doubt. As an artist, his earlier visions of God had come from great works of art: Michelangelo, Blake, El Greco. His conception of God also reflects his Catholic upbringing. When he tells Robert that God is a spirit, "he imagined Him as a vaporous goodness inside people's being" (92). But after he loses his son, Ives' faith, his belief and trust in God, seems to be lost as well. In an attempt to free God of responsibility, Ives tries believing in the God of Deism who "did not interfere in human affairs" (164). But what good is a God who sees all, but who does nothing to prevent evil and suffering? Ives tries to recall his earlier mystical vision, trying to interpret it as a sign of life after death, but he is still filled with doubt. He concludes that the vision was nothing more than "an expression of supernatural folly" (137).

Ives is unable to take comfort in traditional Christian responses to suffering and the problem of evil.

> [T]hough he spoke kindly with the priests and repeated to himself a thousand times that God was good and the manifestations of evil that come to men are ultimately explicable in some divine way, His wisdom greater than what any of them would ever know, Ives felt a great numbness descending over him. (141)

But despite losing the *feelings* that used to animate his faith, Ives continues to be a good man, both in his charity toward others, even his son's murderer, and in his devotion to God, devotion defined not as feelings of deep love but rather as a strong dedication and loyalty, even in the absence of these feelings. Therefore, "despite his doubts," Ives approaches "the whole notion of faith as a matter of will and discipline" (173). He remains devoted to God in prayer, and he continues to use his modest means to help others in his neighborhood.

The same kind of devotion characterizes his relationship with his wife, Annie. Ives continues to be a good and kind husband and father, but his inability to end his grieving for Robert causes a rift in his marriage. As Ives' heart grows cold, he and Annie drift apart, a wrenching development after the story of their passionate courtship. Like Ives, Annie also continues to do good works, working as a teacher in dangerous, inner-city schools, but eventually she grows cynical, stops teaching at these schools— after having her life threatened by students too many times—and loses her belief that the goodness of individuals can really do anything to change the world.

While Annie counsels Ives to get over his grief, his best friend, Luis Ramirez, urges him to seek revenge. Luis insists that God doesn't care about us, and that it is up to us to execute justice. Many in his neighborhood agree, but Ives begs them not to seek retaliation. He goes even further by striving to forgive the boy who has murdered his son. Ives wears out his knees in prayer, beseeching God to grant him the gift of forgiveness, the ability to forgive his son's murderer. Once again, even though he is unable to feel forgiveness for the boy, he nevertheless continues to act as if he has forgiven him, sending him a Bible and letters of encouragement, trying, to the bewilderment of Ramirez, "to convert—to *save*—the soul of Daniel Gomez, his son's murderer" (171). Ives even writes the parole board on behalf of Gomez. Having developed the habits of faith and goodness, Ives continues his charitable acts, even though his own heart is numb. As he struggles with unbelief, habit becomes a placeholder for hope.

Nevertheless, despite a lifetime of goodness, Ives continues to be afflicted with grief. He is unable to be comforted. But as he grows ever more distant from his wife, he once again does the right thing, though perhaps belatedly. He finally agrees to a trip to England with Annie, and during this trip, their love and affection for each other is revived. As his heart softens toward his wife, he receives a dream vision that restores him, physically and spiritually. Like Job scratching at his boils, Ives has developed a habit of scratching at his skin, leaving his skin torn and bloody, as if inflicting penance upon himself, as he contemplates the suffering and stigmata of Christ on the cross. In his dream, Robert, at the age of forty three, the age he would have been had he not died, asks his father why he continues to torment and torture himself, both mentally and physically. Robert then pours water from a stream over his father's skin, and when Ives awakes, his skin has been healed. This baptism by his son, a symbol of death and rebirth, resurrects his faith. Robert, who would have taken on the role of Christ as a priest during Mass, heals his father, much as Christ healed the leper.

Feeling stronger after this healing dream, Ives is nevertheless stunned when a priest calls to inform him that Gomez, his son's murderer, very much wants to meet Ives, whom he has never seen, face to face. At the mention of his son's killer, Ives feels as if a noxious gas had entered the room, but seeking to expel the bitterness that has poisoned his life, Ives agrees to meet with him. During their encounter, Ives is given the power to forgive the man who destroyed not only his son's life, but also much of his own as well. Ives has made every effort to forgive this man, heroically acting as if he feels the forgiveness for which he has so long prayed. But it takes more than human willpower to love such an enemy, and Ives, as he embraces his son's killer, finally receives the grace to forgive, a gift *"from without"* (204) that he has so long desired.

We leave Ives where we first met him, full of emotion, worshiping in church, meditating upon the figure of Jesus. But whereas in the opening scene Ives focuses on the Christ child, here he has a vision of the resurrected Christ, coming down off of the cross to bring all those who have done good to be with him in heaven. As he imagines Christ "placing His wounded hands" upon his brow and taking him to heaven, "with its four mysterious winds" (248), we recall the four swirling winds Ives perceived in his earlier mystical experience and sense with him the completion of a long and arduous journey.

▨ Discussion Questions about the Novel

1. At the very beginning of the novel, we are told that Robert has been murdered. How does this information shape the way we read the entire book, especially Ives' mystical experience before his son's death?

2. How does being an orphan influence the way in which Ives feels and looks at the world? How does Ives' adoptive father help to shape Ives' character and does he, in turn, shape his own children in similar ways?

3. What importance does Ives' mystical vision assume after his near-death experience? Why does it bother him that it doesn't seem explicitly Christian? Why doesn't he tell anyone, especially his son, about the vision? Yet, why does he later describe his vision to his friend's son, Paul (163)? Ives' daughter also has a

mystical vision. How does her vision compare to that of Ives? Does her vision affect the credibility of Ives' vision? How so?

4. Is it possible to understand Mr. Ives' faith as simply a fantasy, a desire to have his wishes come true, to feel safe and protected, as Freud would describe it? Can we explain his vision on Madison Avenue as simply a psychological response to his near-death experience? How do you think you would react to such a vision?

5. How does Ives' image of God change throughout the novel (see pages 56–57, 61, 92, 93, 110–11)? What is his final image of God? How has your image of God changed over time?

6. Ives struggles to understand how God could allow or even cause the death of his son. How does Ives think about the problem of evil (164, 173, 196, 200)? Does he ever successfully develop a theodicy, an explanation of why a loving and powerful God allows evil in the world?

7. As Ives teaches his son about his Catholic faith, he tells him that Jesus "took a human form for a time so that He could better understand human beings and He chose to give His life in a painful way, so that He would know suffering" (73). When Ives pictures his son's body, torn apart by bullets, he suddenly imagines the agony of Christ on the cross (136). What do the sufferings of Christ teach Ives about his own suffering?

8. Why does Ives seek to forgive his son's murderer? Is his desire and ability to forgive Gomez presented realistically, or do you find it too idealistic or sentimental? Could you forgive the murderer of your child? Would you want to?

9. Mr. Ives continues to act with goodness, kindness, and charity toward others after his son's death, despite the coldness of his own heart. He also continues to pray, even though he doubts God's goodness, and at times, even his existence. Why does he do this? What effect does it have on his life?

10. How have you responded to painful events in your life? Was your faith strengthened or weakened? Did you blame God? Do you think expressing anger toward God is a necessary part of the grieving process?

▨ Other Books to Consider

—Book of Job, in the Bible.

> The ancient story of the suffering of an innocent man and his attempt to understand why. False comforters blame Job, as if all suffering is a punishment from God, but Job demands that God come and explain himself.

—Charles Dickens, *A Christmas Carol*. London: Chapman and Hall, 1843.

> Dickens's classic story of the repentance and conversion of the miser Scrooge after visions of the past, present, and future. Hijuelos was influenced by the novel in his writing of *Mr. Ives' Christmas*, and in the novel, Annie loves Dickens and Ives owns a signed copy of an 1867 edition of Dickens's *Pickwick Papers*, stolen from his apartment but then restored by the owner of the inn where Ives and Annie stay in England.

—Umberto Eco, *The Name of the Rose*. New York: Harcourt, 1980.

> The narrator of this historical mystery is taken along with Brother William on an investigation of mysterious deaths that come about,

ultimately, because of threats posed by the work of Aristotle to Catholic theology. But beneath this vivid mystery is the story of a young monk—the narrator—who is forced to confront the blemishes, and the evils, that lie even at the surface of the church to which he clings. His search, he tells us at the novel's opening, is for word and truth, but what he finds in his search is a powerful test that threatens to undo his faith.

—John Updike, *In the Beauty of the Lilies.* New York: Knopf, 1996.

Updike begins this three-part generational story in 1910 and traces the fading away of faith within a family, beginning with its Presbyterian minister who loses faith and becomes an encyclopedia salesman. Unlike Mr. Ives, the minister never regains that faith, and Updike poses the questions, what happens in an individual whose faith has eroded away—and, by extension, what happens to a culture when its faith has evaporated?

THE DREAM LIFE OF SUKHANOV Olga Grushin
(2005)

Synopsis

Anatoly Pavlovich Sukhanov ("Tolya") was born in 1929,
twelve years after the Russian Revolution. His father, Pavel
Sukhanov, disappeared under mysterious circumstances
when Anatoly was still a young boy. During his father's
absence, Sukhanov develops his first taste for art when an old
professor across the hall shares with him the lush beauties
of a book of Botticelli prints—a forbidden pleasure in the
Soviet Union. Sukhanov is entranced. But when the young
Sukhanov and his mother are finally reunited with Pavel
Sukhanov, his father kills himself by stepping out of a fifth
floor window.

As a young man, Sukhanov develops a double life. By
day, he toes the party line and teaches at a state-sponsored
art school; by night, he unleashes his considerable artistic
talent in superb surrealistic paintings. The beautiful Nina
Malinina, enamored of the art as much as the artist,
agrees to marry him. After the authorities identify him as
a subversive artist, however, Sukhanov faces a difficult
decision. His powerful father-in-law, Pyotr Alekseevich
Malinin, can secure him stable—even lucrative—
employment as an art critic for the Communist Party if
Sukhanov will abandon the surrealist methods in which he
truly excels. After a tremendous inner struggle, Sukhanov
accepts the job.

This narrative—from Sukhanov's earliest memory through his thirty-third year—is offered in fragmentary flashbacks and dreams throughout the novel. The primary narrative picks up the story twenty-three years later and tells how Sukhanov loses his job as art critic in 1985. At a retrospective exhibition honoring his father-in-law's birthday, Sukhanov inadvertently offends the Minister of Culture, a slip which causes an avalanche in Sukhanov's professional life. Swiftly, smoothly, and secretly, the higher powers maneuver Sukhanov out of his position. Meanwhile, Sukhanov's cousin Dalevich, who has written an article on Chagall, appears unannounced on Sukhanov's doorstep and spends several days as a house guest. Although the exact motivations and machinations are unclear, Dalevich's article is one factor in Sukhanov's firing.

In the course of the novel, Sukhanov also loses his family. His son, Vasily, draws away from his father in favor of Malinin, hoping to exploit his grandfather's connections more effectively than Sukhanov has done. Ksenya, Sukhanov's daughter, elopes with an underground musician and mystic named Tumanov. And Nina moves to their dacha, asking to live alone for an indefinite period of time. The novel ends with Sukhanov returning to his role as an artist. Relieved of all personal and professional responsibilities, he resolves to move into an abandoned church to resume the artistic career that he has put on hold for twenty-three years.

Note on Russian Names

In addition to first and last names, Russians use a middle name called a patronymic, which is derived from the first name of one's father: Anatoly Pavlovich Sukhanov is the son of Pavel Sukhanov; his own son is Vasily Anatolyevich Sukhanov (although he is never identified as such in the novel). Both the first name and patronymic are used to address someone politely, as numerous speakers do in the formal party scene that opens the novel.

Many Russian surnames appear in feminine form (ending in an *a*) when referring to a female: Sukhanov's mother is Nadezhda Sukhanova (88); his wife is Nina Sukhanova (210).

Russians use numerous diminutive forms of a name to signify various levels of informality, just as the English name James might become Jim, Jimmy, or even Jimbo. One diminutive form of "Anatoly" is "Tolya."

The name "Sukhanov" is pronounced *soo-KHAN-uff*. (The "kh" sound is similar to the "ch" in the German *ich*.)

On the Author

Olga Grushin was born in Moscow in 1971, and as a young child lived in Prague. She returned to Moscow to study art history and journalism, and in 1989 came to the United States to attend Emory University. She currently lives with her family in Washington, DC.

Grushin has published short fiction in several journals, including the *Partisan Review* and *The Massachusetts Review*. *The Dream Life of Sukhanov* is her first novel. Published to enthusiastic reviews in 2006, the book earned several honors in that year, including places on the *New York Times* list of Notable Books of the Year and the *Washington Post Book World*'s Top Ten Best Books of 2006.

Considering the Novel

A little snow bank in the back alley is bleeding rainbows. Lurid oranges and reds, cool greens, and smooth blues ooze confusedly onto the slushy pavement. These are important images in *The Dream Life of Sukhanov*, because they are images of both beauty and loss. Fearful of arrest by the authorities, little Tolya Sukhanov has thrust his art book into the snow in a willful attempt to abandon not just Botticelli but beauty itself, because "beauty is for the bourgeois" (93). As he watches the colors leaking away, he smiles with a sense of relief and satisfaction (115). But he is not alone. A small crowd of children, including the burly bullies from across the hall, is laughing in amazement at the magic snow. In his efforts to bury beauty, Sukhanov has ironically revealed it, freeing it from the dusty confines of a heavy book in an old man's study and spilling it into the public square where it delights even the Morozov boys. It offers a fleeting moment of communal joy before disappearing forever into the ground and gutter.

The snow bank is also important because it is thawing, and *The Dream Life of Sukhanov* is a novel about thaws. The most obvious, of course, is the melting of Sukhanov himself, whose name is derived from the Russian adjective *sukhoi*, which means "dry." Like the English word "dry," *sukhoi* includes connotations of barrenness and, when applied to personalities, coldness. By the time the story begins, in 1985, the young Sukhanov has grown into an emotional and intellectual snow bank, cold and dry. By the end of the novel, however, Sukhanov has lost all that keeps his life cool and rigid—his job, his home, his family. He melts back into the painter that he once aspired to be, reversing the momentous choice he made as a young man.

Because Sukhanov's choice is essentially between different modes of art, it might be best to understand his decision through two different paintings. In chapter five, Sukhanov replaces a mysterious mythological scene painted by his old friend Belkin with a sunny still life by his father-in-law, Malinin. In choosing between the two paintings, Sukhanov repeats his own career choice as a painter, and so the paintings suggest what is at stake for him.

The Belkin painting, given to the Sukhanovs as a wedding present, is the more complex of the two and the one most closely connected to the major themes of the novel. It depicts the scene from Greek mythology in which Zeus assumes the form of a swan in order to seduce the mortal girl Leda:

> A raven-haired girl sat by dark moonlit waters. The luminous curve of her nude body was misty as a dream, even slightly transparent, so that, if one looked very closely, one could just make out pale shapes of water lilies visible through her honey-colored, unearthly flesh. An indistinct silhouette of a youth, perhaps an admiring shepherd, was crouching in the rushes behind her, but she took no notice of him. She was gazing away, over the waters, to a horizon where a magnificent white swan was floating, slowly, majestically, triumphantly, moving closer and closer. (56)

Near the end of the novel, Sukhanov offers a programmatic interpretation of this painting. Nina is the girl, of course, and Sukhanov himself is the mighty swan who seduces her with the powerful beauty of his art. Belkin is the shepherd boy, Nina's "youthful, earthly love," relegated to a place in the weeds as the swan advances (343). For years Sukhanov has wondered why Nina is occasionally distant from him, when in fact he has had the true answer all along. It was contained in this painting (which the Sukhanovs had relegated to a closet).

What makes a painting such as this one true, however, is not a neatly allegorical meaning such as the one Sukhanov offers, but the ways in which it might disturb and provoke a viewer. Allegory is a task for the conscious mind; a painting such as Belkin's attempts to exercise the subconscious. Sukhanov's first interpretation of the picture takes the form of a dream. In his dream, he looks at the girl in the painting and sees Nina. As he gapes, Nina turns and gazes back at him. Sukhanov's own reaction to her gaze mirrors that of the admiring shepherd peering through the rushes: "Frozen in the middle of the room, he felt helpless and suddenly aged in his old-man polka-dot pajamas, dreading the inevitable divine seduction yet unable to turn away" (59). At that moment, however, Nina's role in the painting seems to shift. A ripple runs through her flesh, and she sprouts an enormous pair of white wings. Is she the nude girl? Is she the swan? Or is Sukhanov really the swan? Or the shepherd? Zeus, or an old man in polka-dot pajamas?

Turning away from the painting—he is still in his dream—Sukhanov believes that he has escaped its dizzying swirl of possible messages and returned to his real world. At the windowsill, however, he sees "the real Nina, winged and naked, cautiously trying the temperature of the sky with her big toe" (59). With "maddening fluid grace," she glides into the sky and disappears. This "real Nina" turns out to be yet another figure in Sukhanov's dream. The *real* real Nina appears on the following page, leaning over the railing and listening to the couple quarreling in the apartment below. "The real Nina" is thus a hybrid Nina, halfway between the painting and the flesh and blood wife on the balcony. Her wings come from the painting; her posture comes from the actual woman in an apricot-colored gown listening to noise in the courtyard.

In his dream, Sukhanov uses the Belkin painting to make sense of his own experience—in particular, his relationship to Nina. It might seem that the painting sends him spinning in circles, disorienting rather than clarifying. At some level, however, the hybrid Nina is the truth that Sukhanov does not want to know. Although his wife never really sprouts wings, she does fly away from him by the end of the novel. The winged Nina's leap off the balcony is not entirely a flight of fancy. Some part of Sukhanov knows this, but he has a gift for deliberate forgetfulness, and he consciously avoids thinking about Nina's unhappiness. By disorienting and disabling his conscious defenses, however, the painting renders him receptive to the painful truth.

A work of art such as the swan painting is true in the same way that a dream is true: it conveys a genuine feeling or idea—often drawn from waking experience—but without insisting on a form that is consistent or even plausible. Such art can embody truth, but it is a subtle and shifting truth, not easily grasped or held. Solid facts begin to bend and flow; characters blend and melt into one another. "Maddening fluid grace" is an apt description. This fluidity frustrates Sukhanov; he prefers things cut and dried.

Fluidity is an important concept in *The Dream Life of Sukhanov*, and the waterside scene is just one example of its aquatic imagery. The truth that is expressed through beauty, such as the truth about Nina expressed in the swan, is often associated with images of water. Rainbows appear throughout the story, for instance, and are frequently accompanied by actual rain—as with the multicolored invitation that Belkin hands Sukhanov in the downpour outside the Manège (24)—or by some other form of water, such as a melting snow bank. Much of this water imagery coalesces around Nina: the painting of the swan, as well as the portrait of Nina which the swan painting replaces, in which "a pale-haired young woman in light blue emerged dreamily from the darker blue of the sky or possibly a lake, its colors melting gently into the colors of her dress" (7). Sukhanov first says "I love you" to Nina on a bridge across a shimmery lake; their first kiss occurs in a little rented boat (262). It is no accident that Nina is associated with mermaids (8, 281). She consistently represents the fertile fluidity that Sukhanov lacks.

Most importantly, however, water is what becomes of a cold and dry (*sukhoi*) snow bank when it thaws. It takes the entire novel for Sukhanov to fully thaw, however, and in the meantime he resists the fluid truths offered by the artwork around him. At the end of chapter five, haunted and confused by the truth of the swan painting, Sukhanov replaces Belkin's picture with a bright still life of "perfectly round, red apples" painted by his father-in-law (63). In doing so, he re-enacts his career move, abandoning the deep, elusive truth of surrealism—and the truth of his own quietly troubled marriage—for simple realism. These two schools of painting, realism and surrealism, are doubly important to the novel. Not only do they represent Sukhanov's major aesthetic alternatives, but they help to describe Grushin's own method in the work of art that is *The Dream Life of Sukhanov*.

In the early 1930s the Soviet government established—and ruthlessly enforced—the aesthetic doctrine of socialist realism. Fiction was restricted to predictable narratives about strong, hardworking patriots and proletariats who valued their labor and motherland above all else. The graphic arts—such as those painted by Malinin—tended to propaganda; usually they were portraits of leaders such as Stalin or straightforward portrayals of common laborers and their milieu. Art was to serve the state by demonstrating the healthy success of Soviet communism.

The irony, of course, is that the healthy success depicted by socialist realism was terribly inaccurate: poverty ran rampant; thousands starved. The alleged "realism" of this art was in many ways as unreal as the strange concoctions of Dalí, Picasso, and Chagall (who daringly distorted reality without pretending that they were doing otherwise). Traces of this irony appear in the novel. Malinin, who has made his career depicting simple rural scenes, lives in elegant grandeur in the center of Moscow. Upon entering the Malinin home, the young Sukhanov has "no idea that in the year 1957 anyone in Moscow still lived in such old-fashioned luxury" (275). The exhibition hall where the novel opens, a posh gallery filled with glamorous and influential people, is in fact a souped-up stable. The real horses have been herded out long ago; the only sign of them is in the glowing pictures of them adorning the walls. Realism may be optimistic and compulsively believable, but this does not mean that it is true.

Surrealism, on the other hand, handles real subjects such as horses and people and fiddles, but it presents them in ways that do not pretend to be realistic. Salvador Dalí's melting clocks are surreal, for example: clocks are from the real world, but they are presented in ways that are not real: clocks generally do not melt. Just as realist paintings ironically mask the true plight of the people, however, surrealist art—at least for Sukhanov—has the power to embody truth. Malinin's paintings are beautiful, believable lies; Belkin's paintings tend to tell the ugly truths that Sukhanov does not want to hear, and this kind of truth cannot be neatly framed. It lurks uncomfortably around the edges of his mind, intruding into his waking hours as well as his dreams. In fact, the issue of Nina's emotional departure continues to haunt Sukhanov after the dream itself has evaporated. Readers who have stumbled through his dream of the swan doubtless feel reassured when the old man finally emerges from his fantasy, puts his two feet solidly on the floor, and walks out to the balcony, where a wingless Nina is standing at the railing in perfect obedience to the laws of gravity. Finally, this is real.

But what is happening beneath the floor on which the Sukhanovs stand? The quarrelling couple below is strongly suggestive of the unspoken strains in the Sukhanov marriage. As they listen to the drama, Sukhanov and Nina are in a sense listening to their own subconscious angst. The connection to this couple is made much more dramatic later in the novel with the mistakenly delivered love letter. It eventually turns out that Nina Sukhanova has not received a letter from an anonymous lover, but the sad truth of that letter—that the woman's heart has left the relationship—seems perfectly true of the Nina who has left for the dacha. This heavy truth that Sukhanov senses in the swan painting underlies all of his days; it is not banished by a cheery still life of too-perfect apples.

Like Belkin's painting, Grushin's novel itself works in a mildly surrealist mode, portraying a realistic character, but immersing him in a swirling blend of dreams and reality, past and present. Grushin has meticulously embellished her tale with the same flourishes that one might find in a painting by Chagall or the young Sukhanov. Throughout the novel, Sukhanov repeatedly slips into the world inhabited by the hybrid Nina—part real, part dream. Riding home to Moscow on the train, he lurches forward and smashes a lens of his glasses, making his vision fragmented. "Half of his world was now criss-crossed by a radiant, trembling cobweb. . . . The crack splintered the light into dozens of cubist fragments and imparted a rainbow-tinted brightness to one side of his vision . . ." (255). This is a fitting image of Grushin's own method in the novel, which can be described as cubist. (Cubism is, among many other things, the art of portraying a single object from multiple angles simultaneously.) The young Sukhanov experiments with this approach, "trying to depict both the outside of the cup and its contents in a single image" (126). Grushin accomplishes this feat with Sukhanov himself, showing her main character's external circumstances and internal reveries simultaneously.

In earlier dream sequences, Grushin subtly shifts into Sukhanov's perspective by slipping into the first-person voice. Almost without recognizing it, we as readers have been repositioned inside Sukhanov's head. Later in the novel, Grushin continues to melt his past into his present. Here, however, it is not simply that she continues to manipulate the perspective with pronouns. The events themselves blend almost imperceptibly. The Boris Tumanov concert, for example, reminds Sukhanov of the bohemian gatherings of his own youth, but the event actually happens in his own living room. His old boss at the art school speaks metaphorically of his employment as a passenger train, and he demands a ticket from Sukhanov if he wants to stay on the train—which seems like a metaphor for a certain kind of painting until he realizes that he is actually on a literal train from Bogoliubovka to Moscow, but without a literal ticket (264).

In some of the most suggestive scenes of the novel, however, surrealist art is more than a way to consider the deep truths beneath our feet or the ghosts of our past. It is also an opportunity to glimpse the transcendent truths and hopes for the future that are generally considered the domain of religion. Churches appear throughout the book. In chapter five, the opera music coming from the lower apartment transforms the courtyard into a church, with the Big Dipper as an incense holder and the windows of surrounding walls as glowing icons (61). During the Tumanov concert, it is Sukhanov's own living room that becomes an "oddly churchlike place with smoking incense and dancing candles" (191). *Tuman* is Russian for "fog" or "haze." In this instance, the churchlike aura provides more than a mysterious setting for the story. It directly relates to the points that Dalevich makes to Sukhanov earlier in the novel, as the two cousins debate aesthetic theory over pancakes.

Their conversation will lead them, quite literally, to a small church in the middle of Moscow. Dalevich implies connections between medieval icon paintings and surrealism. His comments on icons would be equally applicable to a surrealist such as Chagall:

What better way is there to portray man's unearthly aspirations, I ask you, than by ignoring irrelevant flesh with its trappings of chiaroscuro and perspective, and presenting instead these floating, pure colors, these insubstantial bodies, these luminous faces. . . ? These works create an impression of a door in our dim, mundane lives, opening for a moment to reveal an ethereal glimpse of heaven, a golden flash of God's paradise. The effect becomes far less wondrous if one dilutes such stark, glowing purity with even the smallest dose of your accurately rendered reality. (119)

To these direct, articulate musings of Dalevich, Grushin adds her own subtle suggestions of the religious power of art. As she has noted, street names are important. The street where Sukhanov was born was then called Rozhdestvensky Passage, which translates as "Nativity Passage" or "Christmas Passage" (327). Sukhanov is from day one identified with Christ, a "compassionate man with a holy mission." Of course, Christmas Street has been renamed by the communists, but even its new name, Lebedinov Lane, bears considerable resonance: it means "Swan Lane." His current apartment is on Belinksy Street, named for an outspoken atheist critic of the nineteenth century, but the cab driver is good enough to point out that it was once called Voskresensky Passage, which means "resurrection." Sukhanov returns to this address in the final pages of the story, using the old name (350). This time, the cab driver asks no questions but takes him directly to Resurrection Road.

Christ was thirty-three when he went to the cross. Sukhanov was thirty-three when he reached the crossroads of realism and surrealism, ultimately making the excruciating decision to turn from his original artistic path. Sukhanov muses on this fact at the Boris Tumanov party (191), and he voices the analogy directly in his conversation with Malinin (297). All of these details provide distinctly Christian overtones to Sukhanov's artistic resurrection at the end of the novel. His new ecstatic artistic vision is littered with biblical imagery, "an amalgamation of biblical truths and the essence of Russia's soul" (346). He returns to the abandoned church in Bogoliubovka (which means "God-loving") to accomplish this vision.

The ending of the novel could easily be read as a double resurrection: Sukhanov resurrects his art, and his art resurrects him. Art is a character in the novel, after all. Sukhanov at one points believes that the meddlesome Dalevich represents art itself; through Dalevich, "art was simply having its revenge" (310). (At the time, Sukhanov believes that he has literally spotted Dalevich in several paintings by Salvador Dalí.) When Dalevich reveals Sukhanov's own early sketches, he does not relinquish his role as the emissary of art. That role simply changes from avenger to that of messenger. He is the strong hand of art itself, reaching through time to pull Sukhanov out from twenty-three years of aesthetic malaise. (Twenty-three also happens to be the number of chapters in the novel.)

The ending of the novel is not, therefore, the simple story of a former painter returning to his craft in order to achieve his natural potential. The truth of the novel is stronger than that. The truth is that beauty cannot be forever buried, that even if it is lodged in a cold, dry place, it will either survive until the next thaw, or it will effect such a thaw all on its own, burning that snow bank from within. Art will out.

To Grushin's credit, she leaves the final interpretation of Sukhanov's character open to interpretation, and she has even provided us with legitimate reasons to question the extent of his resurrection. One way to ask these questions is to test the analogy of Sukhanov to Christ: is Sukhanov's sacrifice truly Christlike?

After all, it is only his role as an artist that is crucified, and—as his mother and father-in-law are quick to remind him—at this point in his life he is not just an artist but a husband and potential father (301, 305). Both Sukhanov and Nina are concerned about his tremendous artistic potential, but there are other factors, too. Their parents (his mother and her father) point to family responsibilities. Belkin suggests that Sukhanov was simply afraid that he would fail as an artist (333)—a suggestion that confirms some of Sukhanov's own thinking (303).

Malinin's words to Sukhanov on this subject ought to be taken seriously, because Malinin is not simply a father-in-law concerned about his daughter's welfare, but he is also a fellow artist. He is able to speak to Sukhanov painter to painter, and when he challenges Sukhanov's analogy to Christ, his words carry some weight:

> A martyr about to make a great sacrifice? Except that Christ sacrificed himself for the people. For what would you sacrifice yourself . . . ? For some vague notion of Art with a capital A? Because let me tell you, Anatoly, the Russian people do not need you and your art. . . . *My* kind of art is what our people love. It may not be as amusing as some fantasy by Chagall, but when millions of tired, unhappy men and women want to find a bit of light, hope, or encouragement at the end of their hard day, they would rather look at paintings of the heroic past and harmonious future than puzzle over some portrait of a man with an upside-down green face. (298)

Perhaps these comments make Sukhanov appear even more like Christ, who, according to St. Paul, ". . . did not count equality with God a thing to be grasped, but emptied himself, taking the form of a servant . . ." (Philippians 2:6–7). Sukhanov puts aside his godlike artistic potential, choosing selflessness over selfishness, emptying himself in service to his bride and children. However, the nonartistic aspects of Sukhanov's life complicate the picture. He may humble himself as an artist, but in no sense does he take the form of a servant. On the contrary, he quickly assumes an impressive amount of power, prestige, and comfort. He simply trades the divinity of the artist for the secular divinity of a high-ranking Soviet bureaucrat. His resurrection is also complicated by the image of a self-indulgent artist. Sukhanov scurries off to a forgotten church to conduct lavish artistic experiments in complete isolation. Malinin's words are relevant here: this sacrifice has no meaning for anyone but Sukhanov himself; this move does not suggest interest in art "for the people." Although Sukhanov ends the novel heading to an old Russian church to make paints and pigments out of real Russian soil, his own artistic ambition seems to ignore the communal nature of the Russian soul.

It is important to remember that Sukhanov's decision to abandon art at the age of thirty-three was not the first time that he made this decision. His first artistic awakening comes with the Botticelli book, but Botticelli is soon sacrificed to the party line ("beauty is for the bourgeois"). His second artistic awakening happens in the late fifties, during the so-called Krushchev Thaw, when the government temporarily relaxed censorship and briefly tolerated artistic experimentation. The awakening in the novel, which occurs at the beginning of the Soviet *glasnost* era, is thus Sukhanov's third thaw. It is possible only because his earlier thaws did not last. Ultimately, freezes and thaws in *The Dream Life of Sukhanov* are a chilly reminder that the great personal regeneration described in this novel is far from final.

▨ Discussion Questions about the Novel

1. The characters Malinin and Belkin embody the paths open to the thirty-three-year-old Sukhanov. Do you think that Sukhanov made the right choice given the information and experience he had? Have you benefited from anyone's Sukhanovian sacrifice of talent, interest, or ambition? Have you made such compromises yourself?

2. Sukhanov replaces the swan painting with the still life because he finds Belkin's painting troubling—and perhaps even threatening. In what ways do his reasons for replacing this painting differ from his reasons for turning to socialist realism as a young man? In other words, how does the young Sukhanov's attitude toward surrealism differ from his attitude toward surrealism as an older man? What accounts for these differences?

3. Throughout the novel, birds and flight are associated with people and ideas Sukhanov is attempting to suppress. Dalevich gives Sukhanov's mother a bird in a cage (44). Birds appear near the little church in Moscow (123) and inside the abandoned church at Bogoliubovka (241). Perhaps most important, however, are the birds associated with Sukhanov's father. The pigeons in the park remind Sukhanov of seeing Tatlin's flying machine (50) with Pavel Sukhanov, whose motto was "Don't let anyone clip your wings" (141). How do these images help you understand who Sukhanov is?

4. In the novel, truth tends to be associated with water imagery and with the constantly shifting, subjective experience of surrealist painting—in contrast to the dry certainty of Sukhanov's life, work, and personality. Are there instances

in your own life where truth has proven more fluid than you at first imagined it to be? Have you experienced any thaws, where a cold, dry certainty about someone or something melted like a snow bank?

5. In the early chapters of the book, Nina's physical beauty is emphasized repeatedly—both through the reactions of others and in Sukhanov's own inward reactions to her. At the dacha, however, Sukhanov finds himself face-to-face with a real flesh-and-blood Nina (236). How might we explain the difference between this Nina and the idealized one of the early novel? Has Nina herself put aside some of the glamour of her posh, big city life, or is it Sukhanov's perspective here that has changed?

6. Face-to-face with a grizzled stranger in the abandoned church, Sukhanov feels "unaccountably certain that if he remained with this mysterious man, in this deserted church, for just a while longer, he might in time be able to understand the precise nature of things, to decipher their eternal riddle, to finally read sense into this day, this week, this life—to see clearly, as never before" (245). In the next paragraph, however, he feels a sudden impulse to flee. Is terror an understandable response to truth? Are there times in your life when the nearness of some great truth has frightened you away from discovering what that truth was?

7. Re-entering the abandoned church at the end of the novel, Sukhanov stumbles across the bag he thought had been stolen on his trip back to Moscow (353). Perhaps this is simply an insignificant detail, but the novel invests so much significance in other small details that it is worth asking what

the reappearing bag suggests. How might we interpret this rediscovery? Are there other small, mysterious details that seemed significant to you?

8. Sukhanov's artistic resurrection at the end of the novel comes after he has lost his job, his children, his wife, and his home. Would any one of these losses have been sufficient to trigger his internal revolution, or does it take the combined force of several of them? Do you find his final artistic zeal sincere, or is it merely a way for him to escape the reality of—and perhaps responsibility for—these losses?

Recommended Viewing

These paintings by Marc Chagall are excellent companion pieces to the novel:
- *Above the Town* (1914–18). Trevakov Gallery, Moscow.
- *Self-Portrait with Muse* (1917–18). Private Collection, St. Petersburg.
- *The White Crucifixion* (1938). Art Institute of Chicago.

Other Books to Consider

—Fyodor Dostoevsky, *The Idiot*. London: Heinemann, 1913.

> Prince Myshkin is Dostoevsky's attempt to portray a "perfectly beautiful man." He is Christlike in his honesty and compassion, and therefore completely out of his element in high society. In tracing his story, the novel explores the conflicts between transcendent ideals and the realities of life. A central question of the novel is "What if Christ were only a man?" The question is posed in part by Holbein's graphic painting *Christ's Body in the Tomb*.

—Arthur Miller, *Death of a Salesman*. New York: Viking Press, 1949. First presented on stage in 1949.

> When Willy Loman finds that his career is declining—in fact, he will soon be fired—and that his children Biff and Happy are disappointments, he confronts the fact that perhaps, after all his dreams, his life is without meaning.

✓ —Chaim Potok, *My Name is Asher Lev*. New York: Knopf, 1972.

> When a young boy born in Brooklyn feels the first stirring of a calling to a life as an artist, he has little idea of the conflicts that will arise: with his father, who is appalled at his son's throwing away of a heroic history and future; with this mother, who is torn between the dreams of her husband and son; and with his own religious culture, from which he must break if he is to fulfill his artistic dreams.

—Leo Tolstoy, *The Death of Ivan Ilyich*. New York: George Munro, 1888.

> Ivan Ilyich has lived his life properly, with the right career, the right wife, the right house—all designed to show those around him that he has made the proper choices. But in making them, he has stilled other voices that might have led to other paths, paths not defined by proper approval, but paths that might have shown the richness of life. Now, dying, Ivan Ilyich is surrounded by pretense and illusion, broken only by the servant boy Gerasim, who understands that death is part of life. Only at the end, when Ivan Ilyich resolves to set his family free from illusion and its pains, does he move toward real life.

Integrative Discussion Questions
for Part Four

1. Novels of initiation generally show characters who come from one situation—often a very protected situation—who then encounter changes and difficulties in new circumstances which lead to both tension and, ultimately, to growth. Godric, Ives, and Tolya all enter situations that are new to them. These situations are governed by certain rules and customs that have to do with what behavior is acceptable and not acceptable, what routines order the day, what kinds of personal growth are to be encouraged, what work is valued or not valued. What similarities do you find in the approaches of Godric and Ives and Tolya to their new worlds?

2. All three novels in this section present characters who are awakened to God or to spiritual realities through extraordinary experiences. Yet each also wrestles with the meaning of these experiences and doubts their reality. What is the role of visions and the miraculous in the life of faith? Do such encounters produce as much doubt as confidence? What has been your own experience with the unexplained?

3. Godric, Ives, and Tolya all pursue daily routines that help them make sense of their lives. Godric's ascetic rituals remind him of his sin even as he seeks to purge it from both body and memory. Ives finds the forms and formulas of faith comforting even when his faith is weak or nonexistent. Toyla buries himself in the routines of his socialist career in an attempt to keep at bay thoughts of his past and recognition of his current failures. What roles do the forms and formulas of faith play in our lives? How might those roles be most authentic?

Integrative Discussion Questions about the Novels

1. How do the stories in novels function as real spiritual disciplines for us? In both *Godric* and *Peace Like a River*, the reader is asked to accept the presence of the miraculous within the common world. In *Mariette in Ecstasy* and *Mr. Ives' Christmas*, the authors craft their narratives to place the very ordinary and commonplace immediately beside the miraculous and ecstatic. In *Life of Pi*, the miraculous stands beside the extraordinary. How might stories such as these wake us up to the presence of God in a world that focuses on the ordinary and the glitzy?

2. Imagine the characters of our novels in conversation with each other. In *The Sparrow* and *The Children of God*, Father Sandoz is faced with the possibility of a God who does not respond to real needs, even when the needs are generated out of obedience. By the end of the first novel, Sandoz has in fact lost his faith. In *Mariette in Ecstasy*, Mariette too looks for a withdrawal of Christ from her life, and suggests that this withdrawal is a testing and issues from Christ's true love for her. Mr. Ives also struggles with the uncertainty of hearing God's voice, as the death of his son seems so unreasonable and random. Dottie, in *This Heavy Silence*, imagines God as distant, disapproving, and unapproachable, and even Godric rarely experiences Christ's presence. If these characters were in conversation about the issue of God's silence, how might they respond to each other?

3. How might the boundaries of a novel genre affect the way spiritual meanings are presented in it? Compared to novels

with a strong historical framework such as *Atonement* or *Mr. Ives' Christmas* or *Snow Falling on Cedars*, novels such as *Life of Pi* and *The Children of Men* seem closer to works of science fiction, such as *The Sparrow* and *The Children of God*. How do the expectations that we have as readers regarding the rules and boundaries of a genre affect our reading? Do these expectations constrict us? Do they provide something for the author to use? Does a less familiar genre, like the graphic novel format of *Road to Perdition*, help us become more aware of the ways genre shapes us as readers?

4. Can a writer successfully depict a saint who is true to life? What exactly makes a person a saint? *Mariette in Ecstasy*, *Godric*, *The Sparrow*, *Mr. Ives' Christmas*, *Peace Like a River*, *Road to Perdition*, and *Life of Pi* present characters with a deep longing for God; in fact, this longing seems to make them saintly. In contrast, in what ways might Kabuo Miyamoto in *Snow Falling on Cedars* or Stanley in *This Heavy Silence* be considered saintly? Which of these "saints" appeals to you the most: Mariette, Godric, Father Emilio Sandoz, Mr. Ives, Jeremiah Land, Michael O'Sullivan, or Pi? Which seems most true to life?

5. Most of the novels here depict relationships between parents and children. In some cases, the parents fail their children in spectacular ways. Godric's father, Aedlward, is all but absent from Godric's life, working in the fields in order to sustain his family. Briony Tallis's father, Jack, is altogether absent from *Atonement*. Dottie fails to establish an emotional bond with Mattie. Dr. Baptiste abuses his daughters. At other times, parents are simply unable to protect their children or to bond to them in meaningful ways; here we think of Michael

O'Sullivan, Mr. Ives, Mr. and Mrs. Patel, Tolya, Father Sandoz, even Jeremiah Land. Why is the parent/child theme so prevalent and powerful in novels? Do these novels speak to your experience as a parent or a child?

6. Many characters in these novels suffer greatly and react in very different ways to their suffering. What in their personalities, habits, and faith determines how they will respond to suffering?

7. Is it fair to say that fiction is able to show us spiritual truth? Are there tensions in using fiction to depict truth—any kind of truth?

Acknowledgments

The Emmaus Readers might never have existed but for the creative mind of our editor, Jon Sweeney, at Paraclete Press. "Wouldn't you like to write a guide for book club readers?" he asked Gary one snowy, January day. "No," thought Gary, but the question niggled and nagged and finally formed itself into this idea: it would be fun to gather some friends together to read and talk about contemporary novels.

We were a diverse—if not motley—crew. Chad Engbers, who has studied the writings of Frederick Buechner ever since hearing him speak in the early nineties, teaches British and Russian literature. He wrote the essays on *Godric* and the *The Dream of Sukhanov*. Susan Felch teaches English and usually spends her days among the writers of the sixteenth century, so she was happy to write one essay on a contemporary British novel, *Atonement*, and another on a Midwestern American novel, *This Heavy Silence*. Brian Ingraffia, who teaches English and is particularly interested in recent novels written by Hispanic, African-American, and African writers, wrote the essay on *Mr. Ives' Christmas*. Glenn Remelts, head librarian at Calvin, keeps his mind clear with backcountry hiking trips. He brought his interest and expertise in science fiction to the essay on *The Sparrow* and *The Children of God*. Gary Schmidt, who teaches English and loves New England, expanded his reach with essays on two novels written by West Coast authors: *Mariette in Ecstasy* and *Snow Falling on Cedars*. Otto Selles, a Canadian who teaches French and reads English language fiction and poetry as much as he can, wrote the essays on *The Life of Pi* and *Peace Like a River*. Cynthia Slagter teaches Spanish, but her guilty pleasure is reading British mystery novels. She wrote the essay on *The Children of Men*. Jeff Tatum, who teaches sociology, tested out early drafts of several essays with friends he has kept in contact with since early graduate school days. Jennifer Hardy Williams, who teaches English, first encountered the narrative power of words and pictures together by reading her father's vast comic book collection when she was a young girl. She contributed the essay on *The Road to Perdition*.

We were encouraged along the way by the hospitality of Calvin College colleagues, particularly Shirley Roels, who provided money for books and snacks through the Lilly Vocation Project, and Jim Bratt, director of the Calvin Center for Christian Scholarship, which subsidized this project with a grant.

As editors, our own deep thanks, as always, is to Doug and Anne.

Susan M. Felch and Gary D. Schmidt

Bibliography

Page numbers in the text refer to the following recent editions of the novels:

—Frederick Buechner, *Godric* (San Franciso: HarperSanFranciso, 1983).

—Max Allan Collins, *Road to Perdition,* illustrated by Richard Piers Rayner (New York: Paradox Press, 1998).

—Leif Enger, *Peace Like a River* (New York: Grove Press, 2001).

—Olga Grushin, *The Dream Life of Sukhanov* (New York: G.P. Putnam's Sons, 2005).

—David Guterson, *Snow Falling on Cedars* (New York: Vintage Books, 1995).

—Ron Hansen, *Mariette in Ecstasy* (New York: Harper Perennial, 1992).

—Oscar Hijuelos, *Mr. Ives' Christmas* (New York: Harper Perennial, 1996).

—P.D. James, *The Children of Men* (New York: Vintage Books, 2006).

—Yann Martel, *Life of Pi* (New York: Harcourt, 2001).

—Nicole Mazzarella, *This Heavy Silence* (Brewster, MA: Paraclete Press, 2005).

—Ian McEwan, *Atonement* (New York: Anchor Books, 2003).

—Mary Doria Russell, *Children of God* (New York: Fawcett Books, 1999).

—Mary Doria Russell, *The Sparrow* (New York: Ballantine Books, 1997).

Also Available

This Heavy Silence

ISBN: 978-1-55725-508-2
250 pages
$14.95, Paperback

Featured in
The Emmaus Readers

- *Winner* 2006 Christy Award
- *Winner Christianity Today* Book Award

When Dottie adopts her best friend's daughter out of a combination of spite and loyalty, she must confront her own ideas on motherhood, loneliness, love, and God.

Saving Erasmus

ISBN: 978-1-55725-498-6
220 pages
$21.95, Hardcover

Named one of the "Top Ten Christian Novels of 2007" by both ALA *Booklist* and *Publishers Weekly*

"Readers looking for something fresh
and a little different from the usual
heavyhanded fare in spiritual fiction will
enjoy this slim novel.
Highly recommended."
—*Library Journal*, starred review

Available from most booksellers or through Paraclete Press
www.paracletepress.com | **1-800-451-5006**
Try your local bookstore first.